This Comic Book for Minecrafters Belongs To:

____

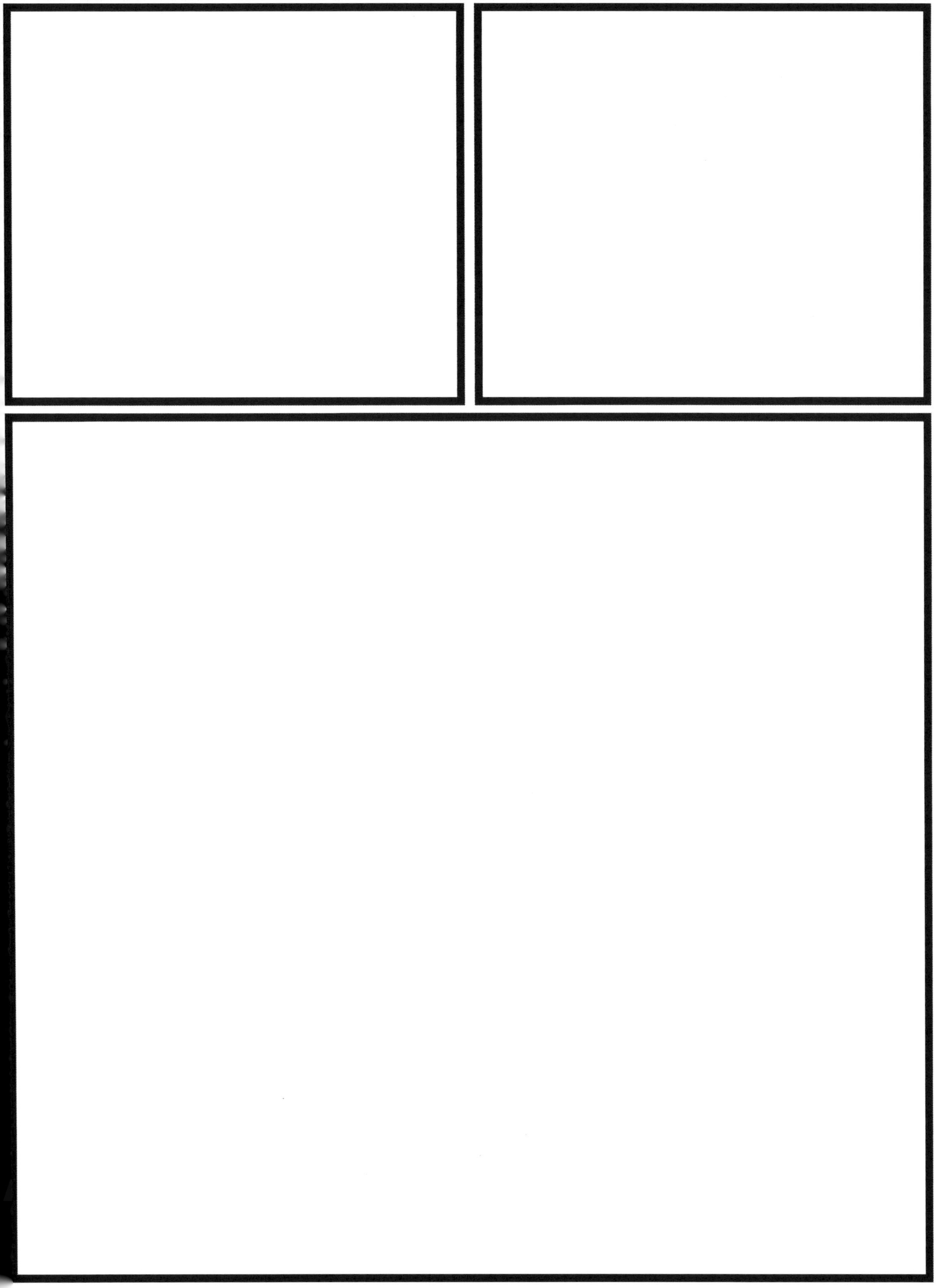

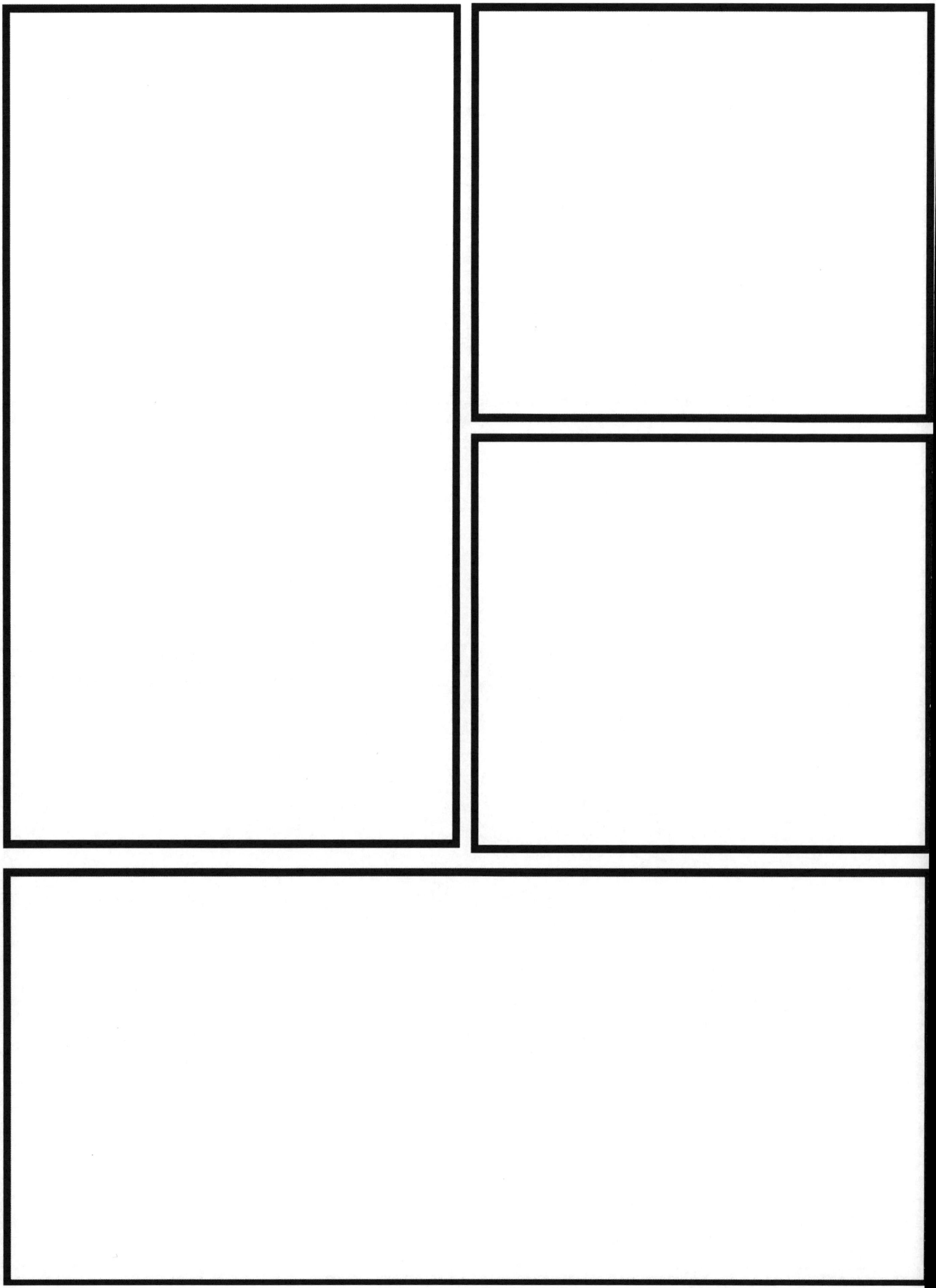

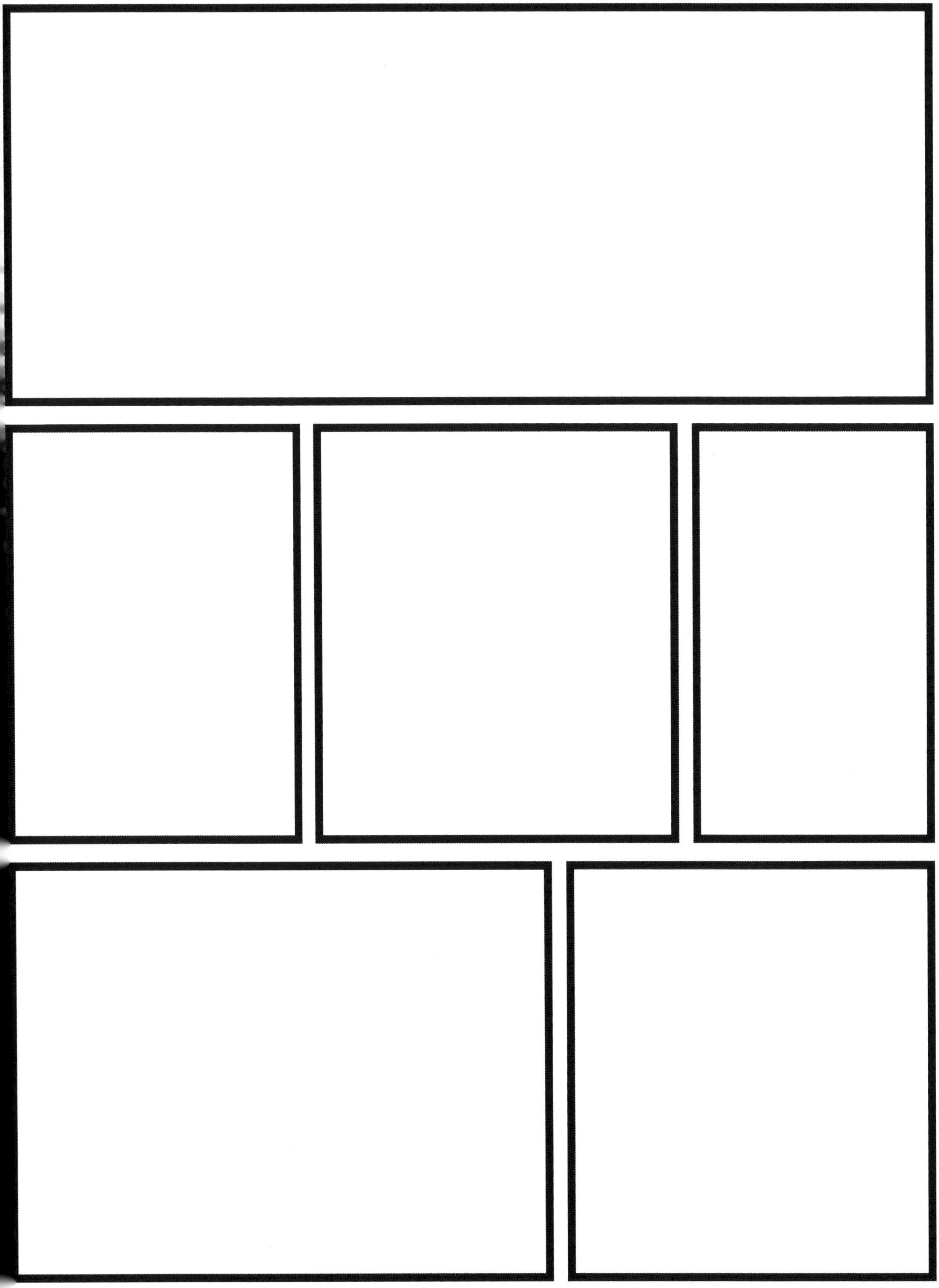

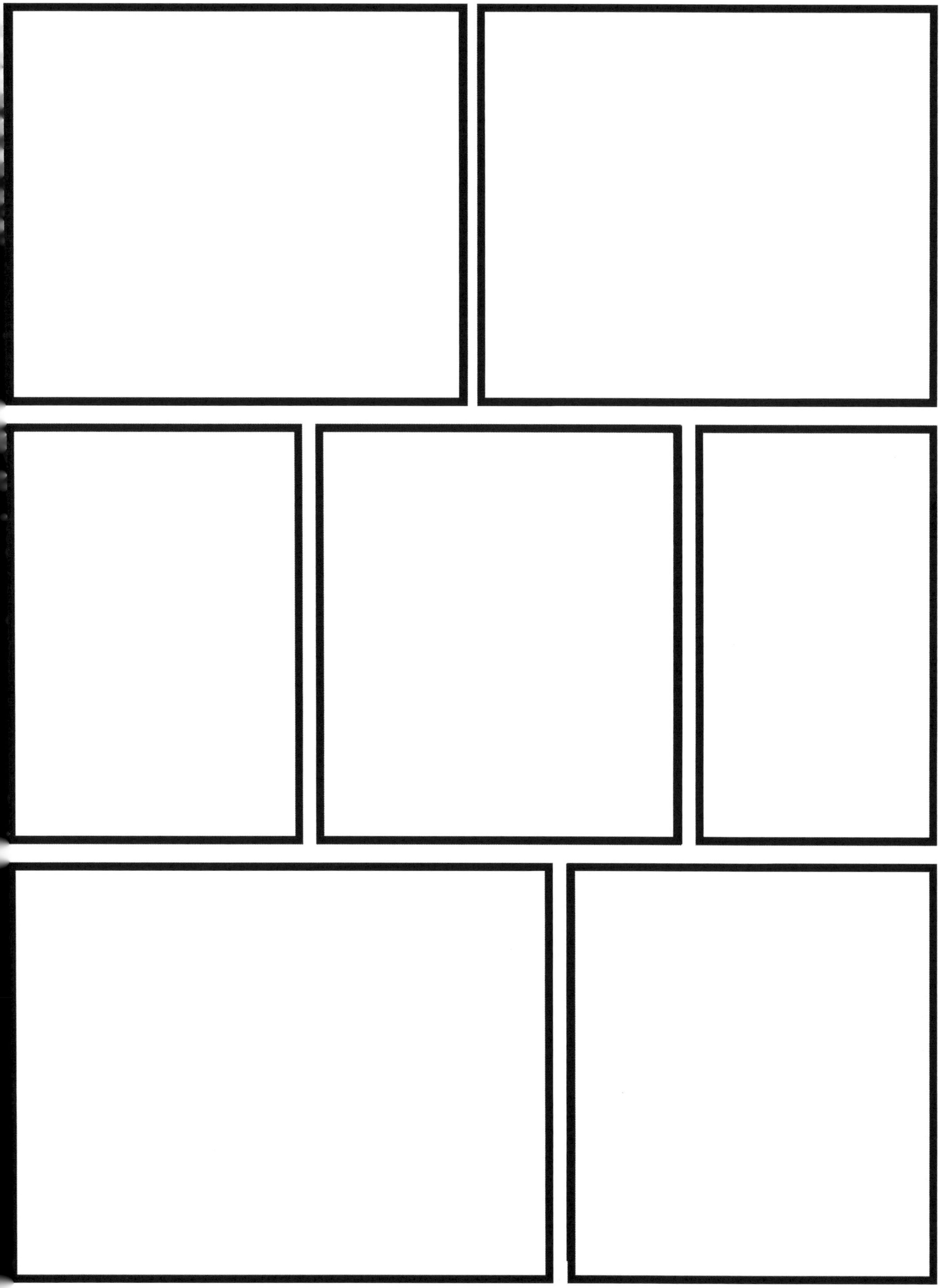

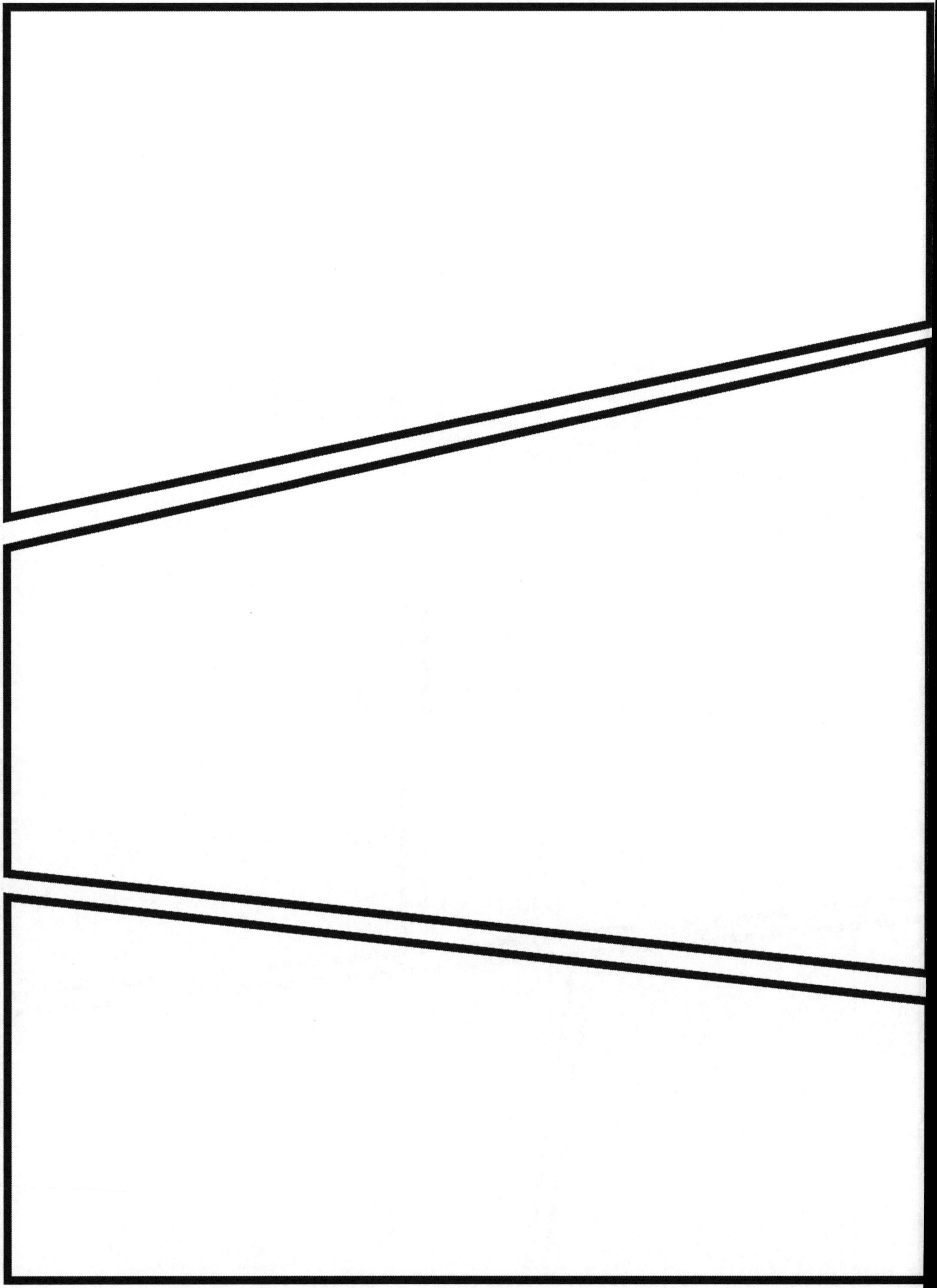

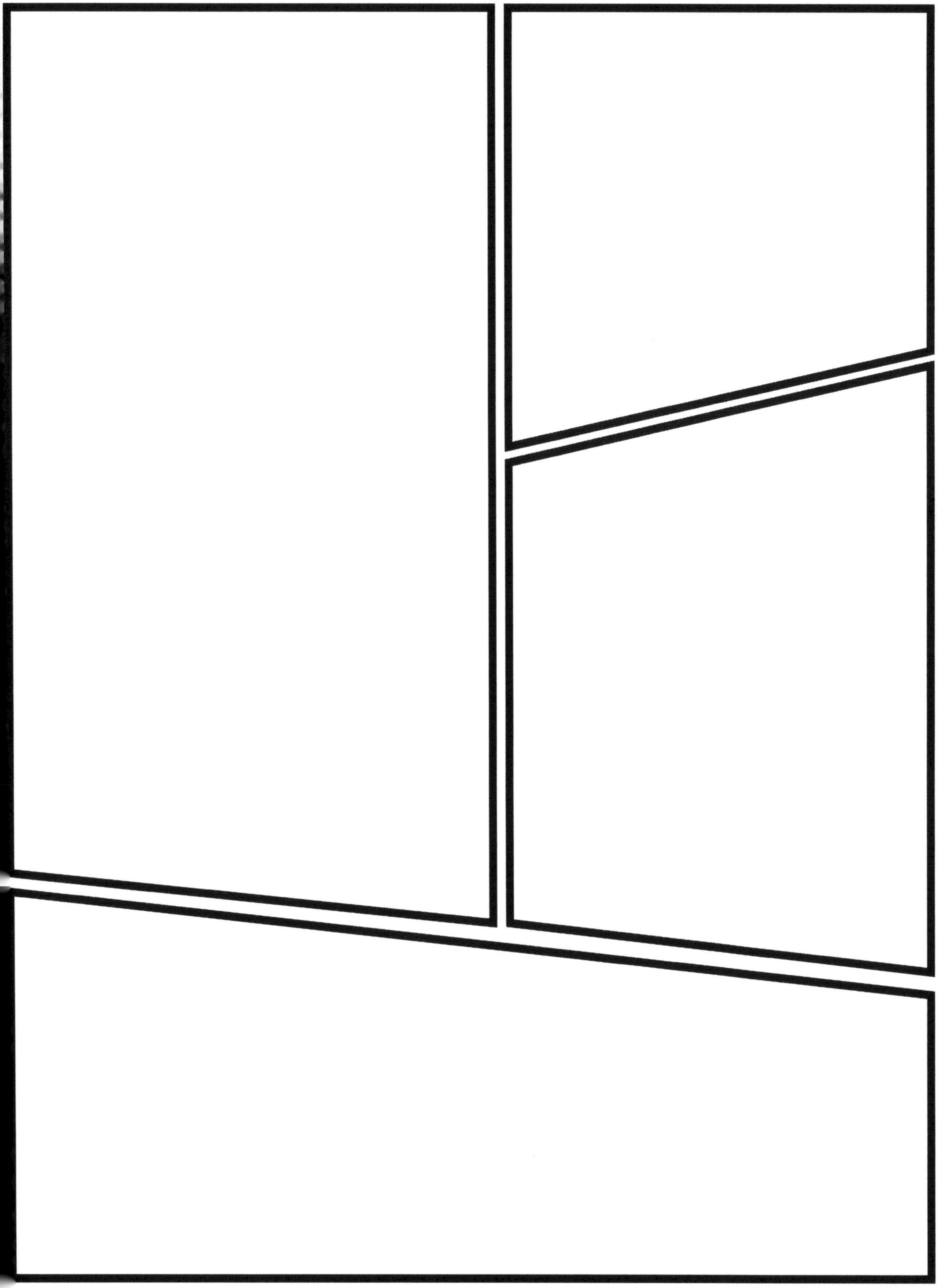

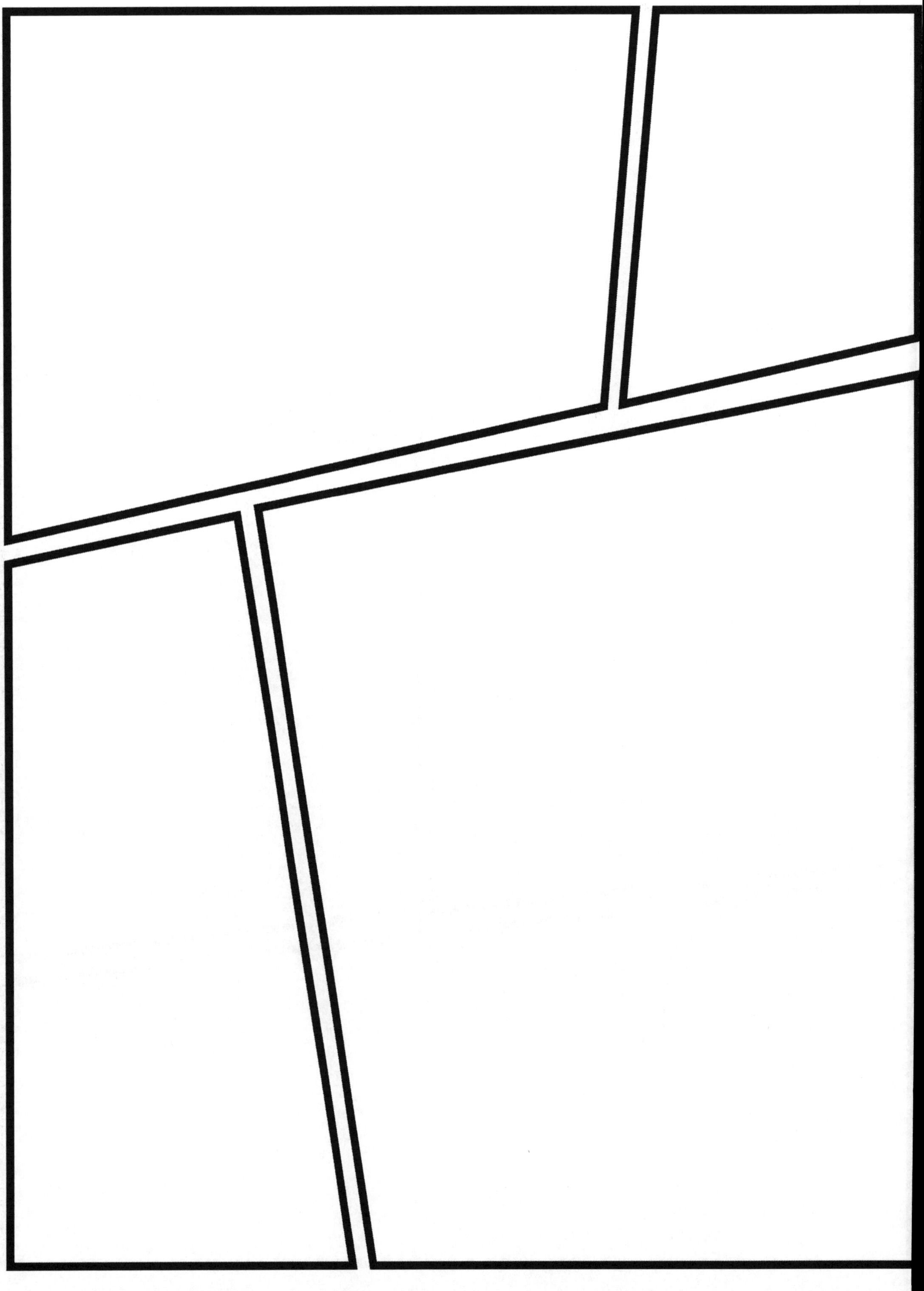

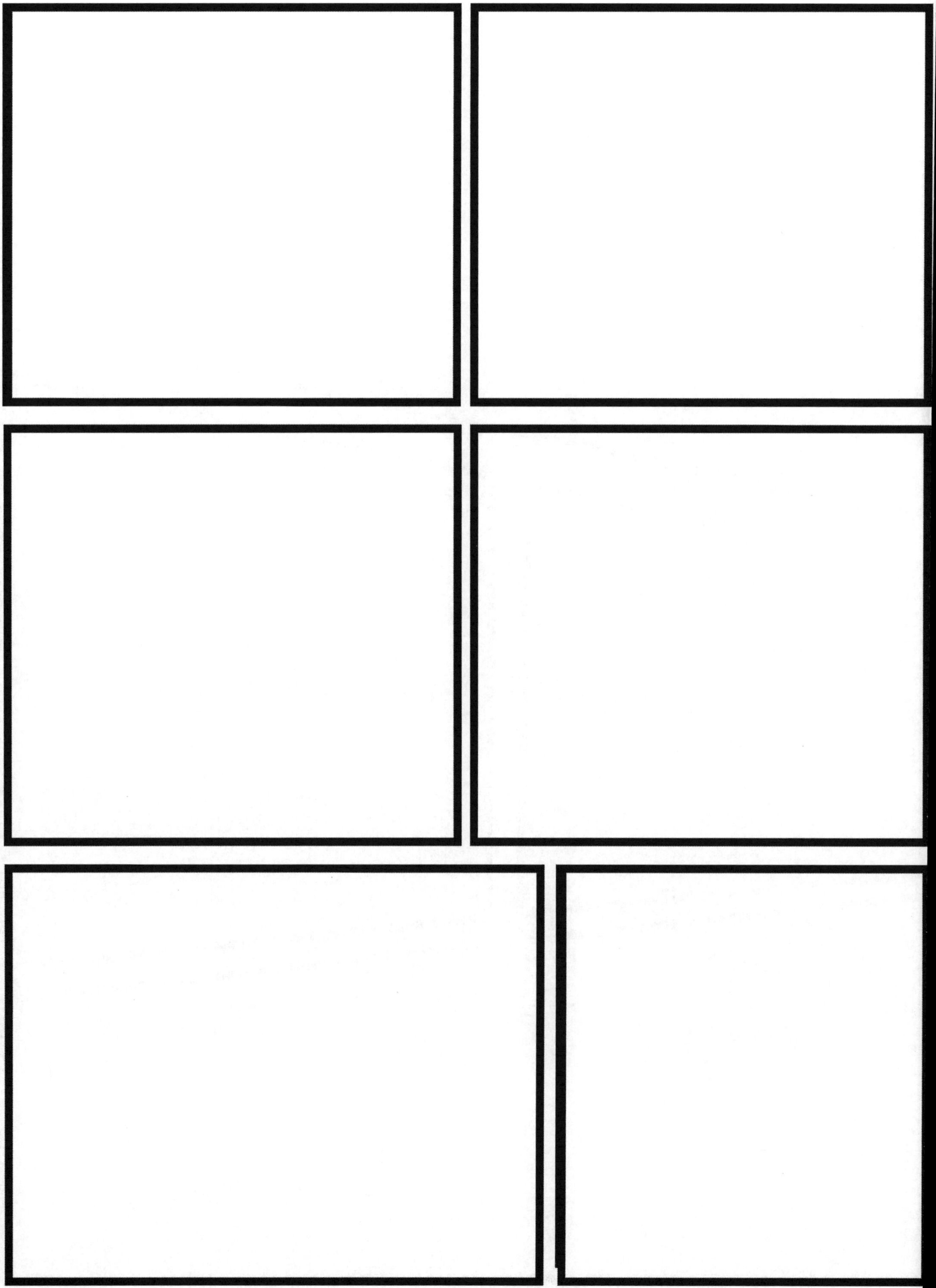

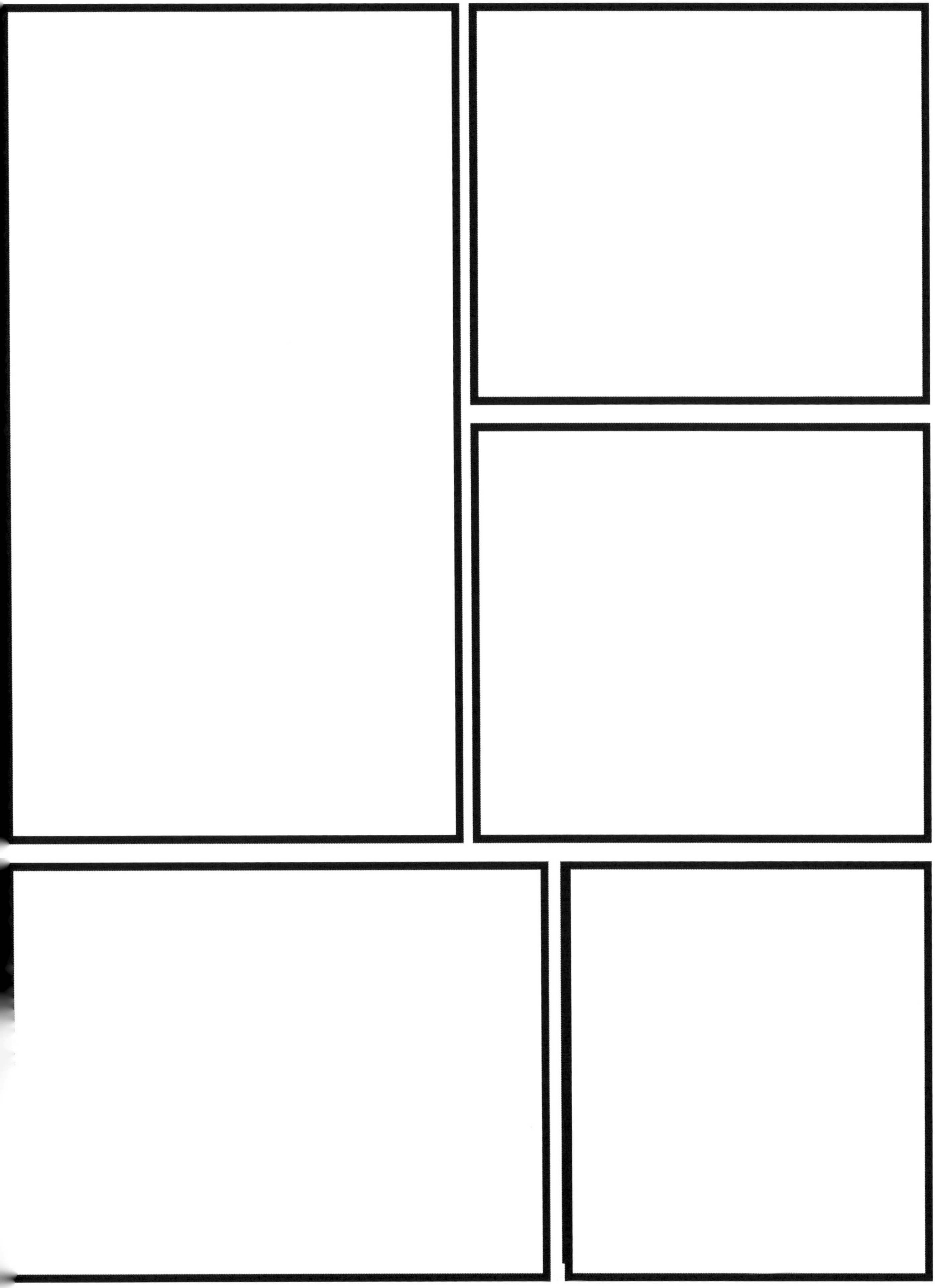

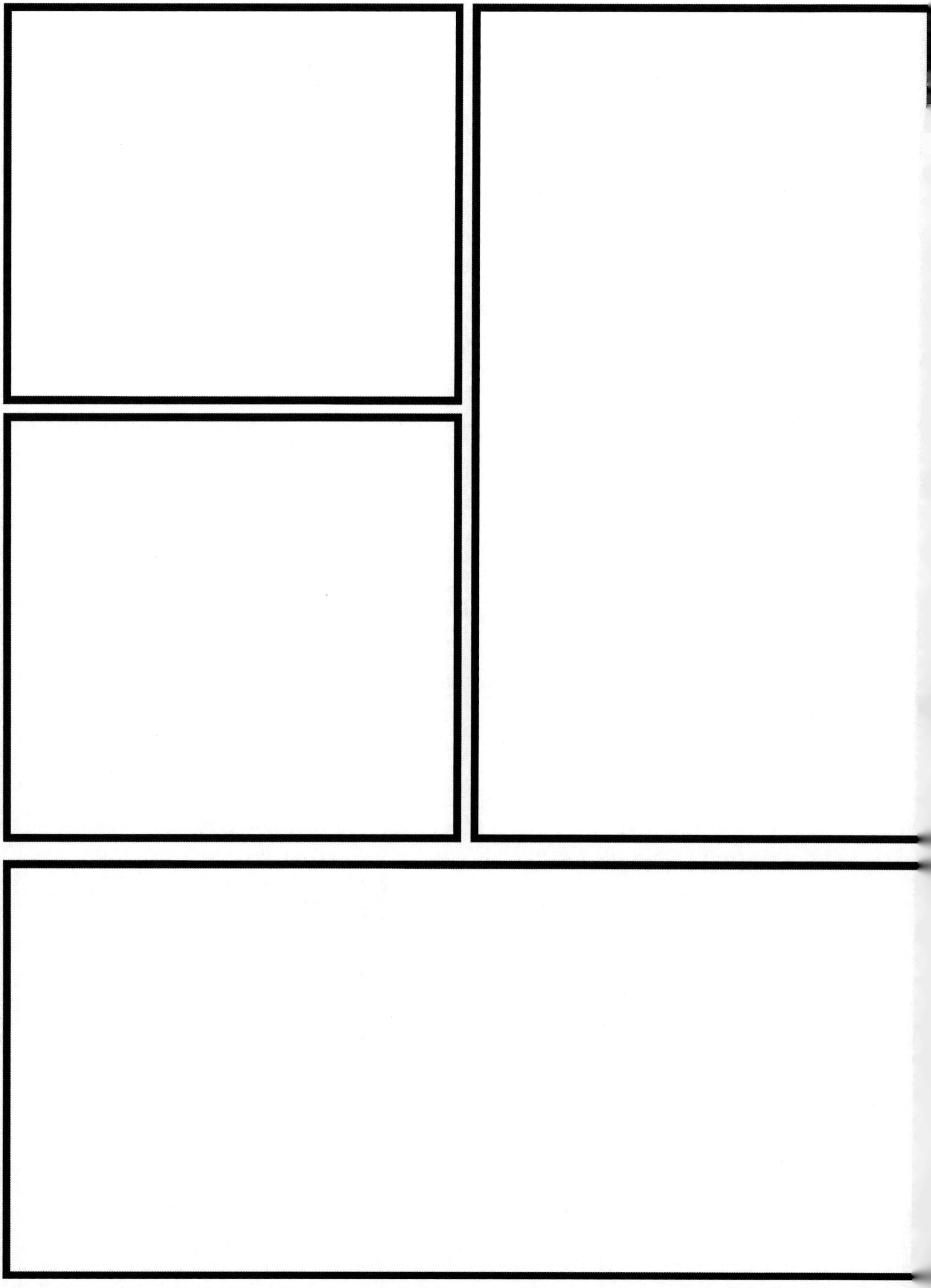

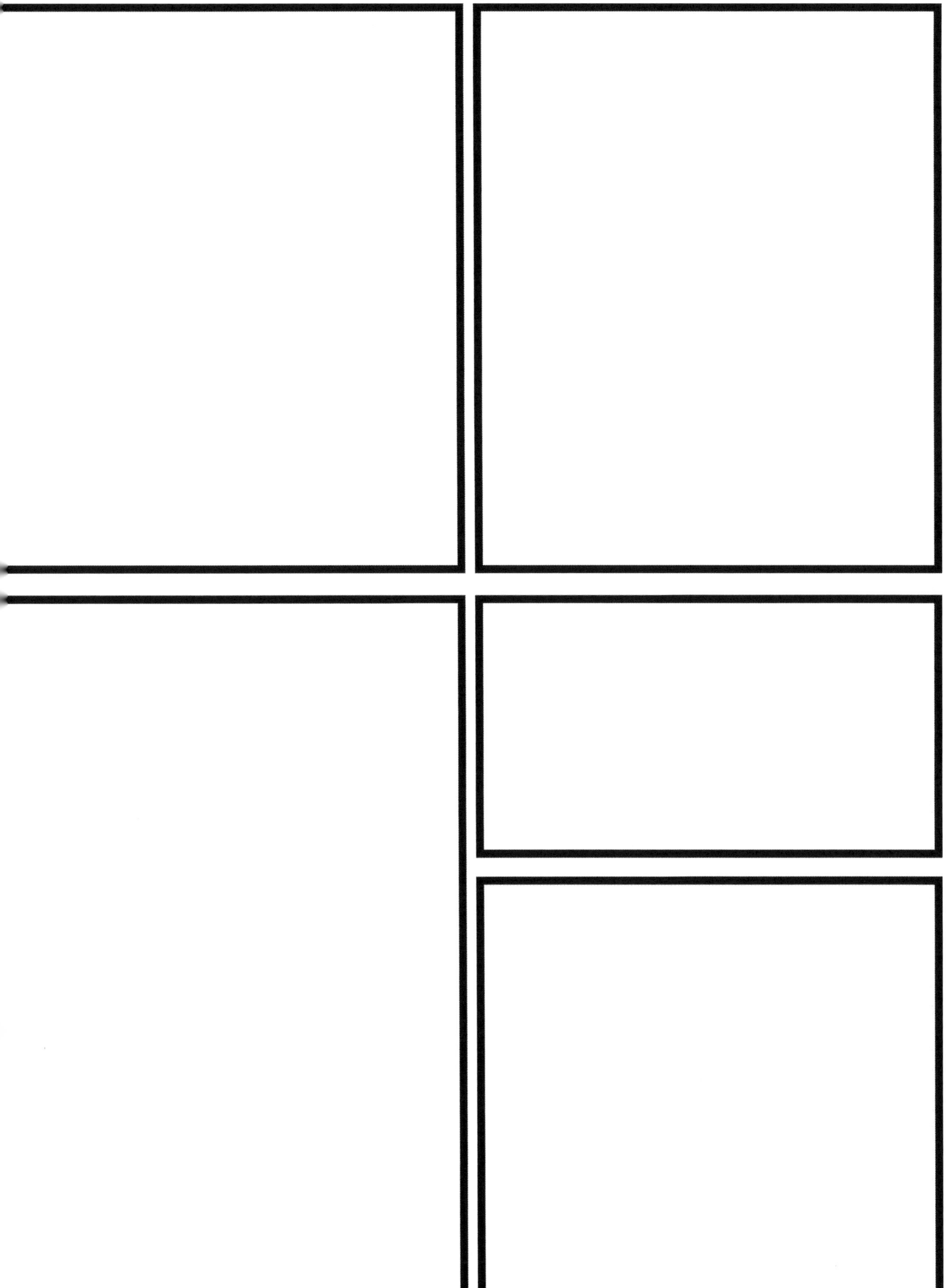

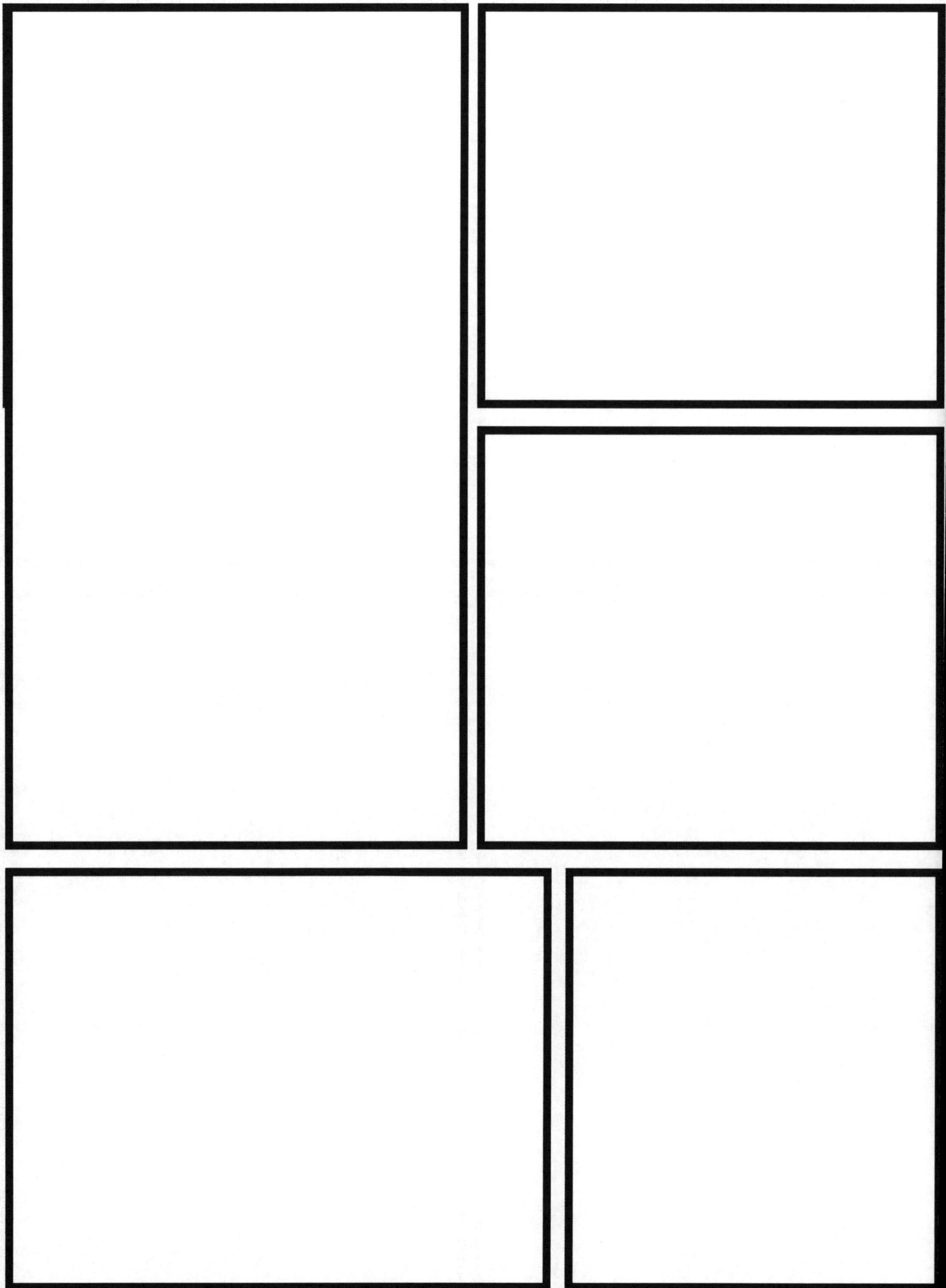

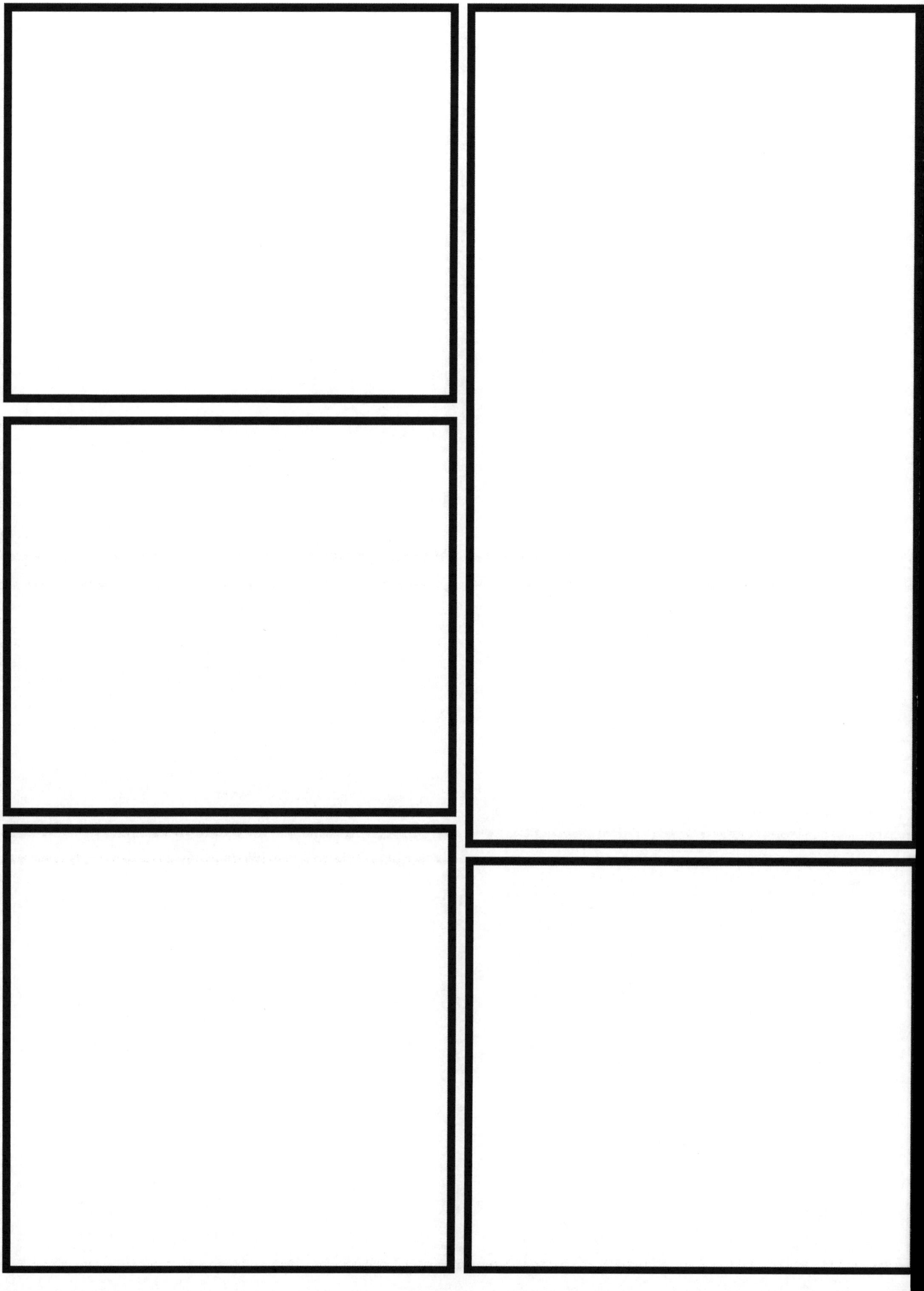

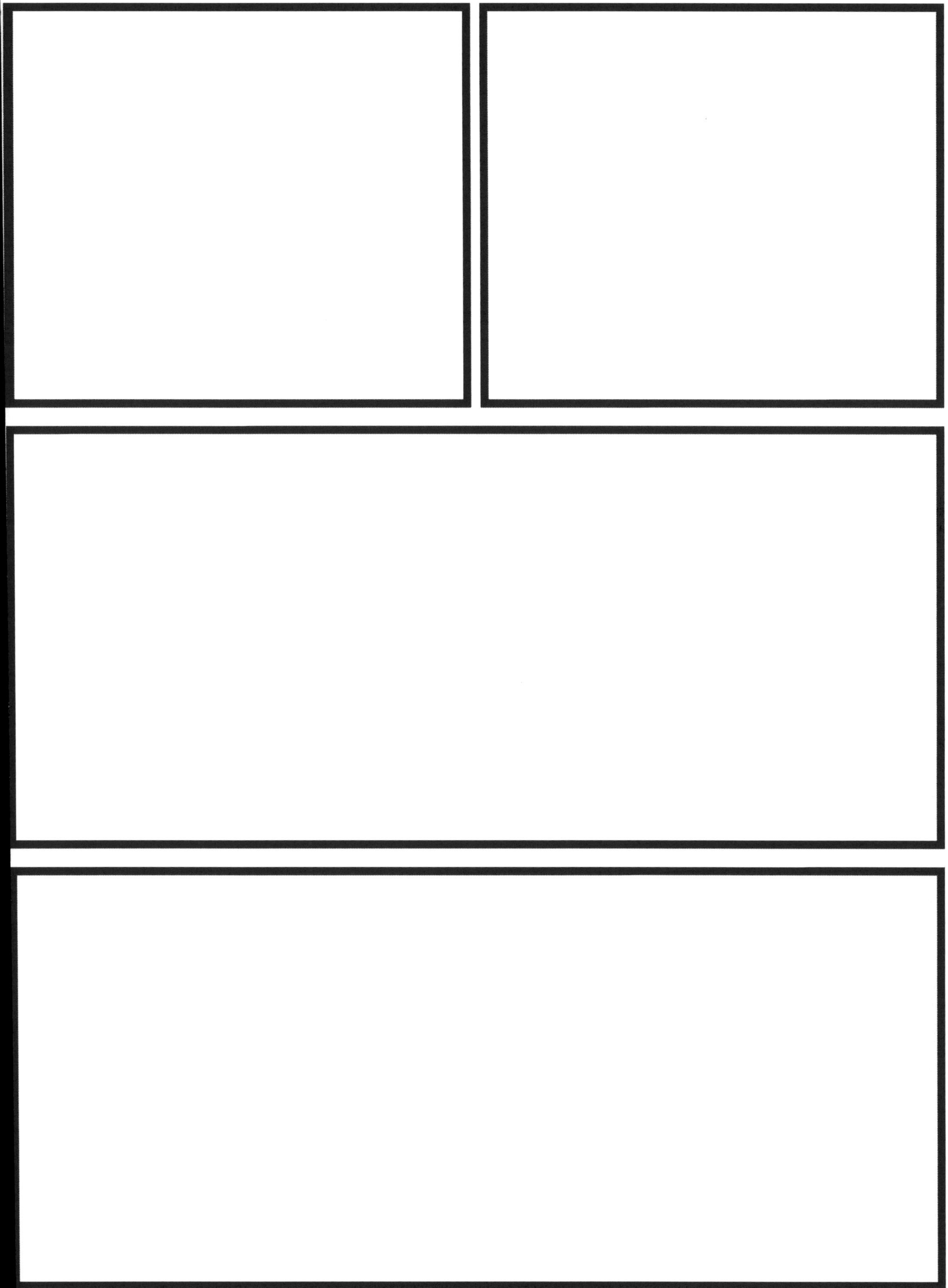

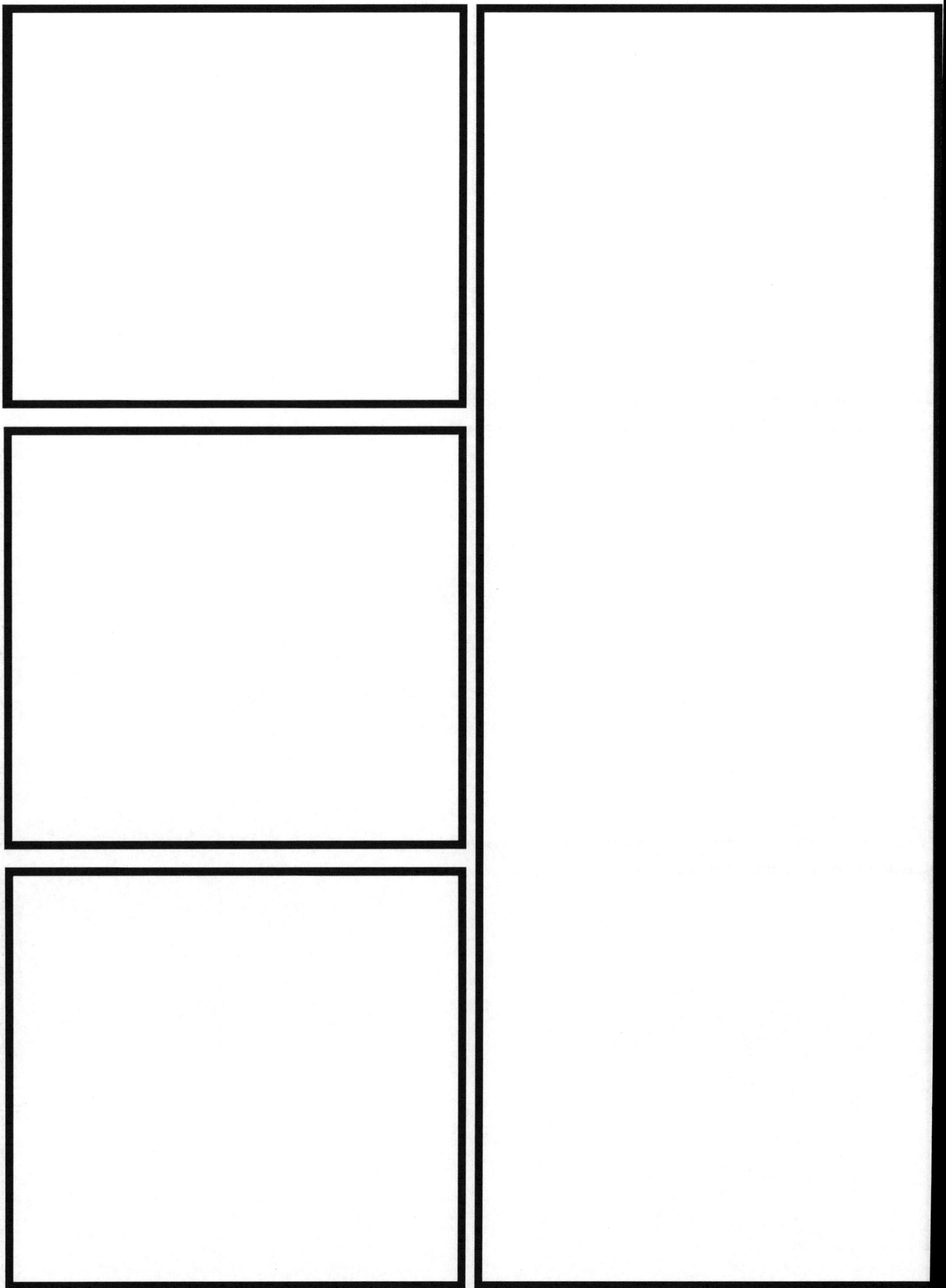

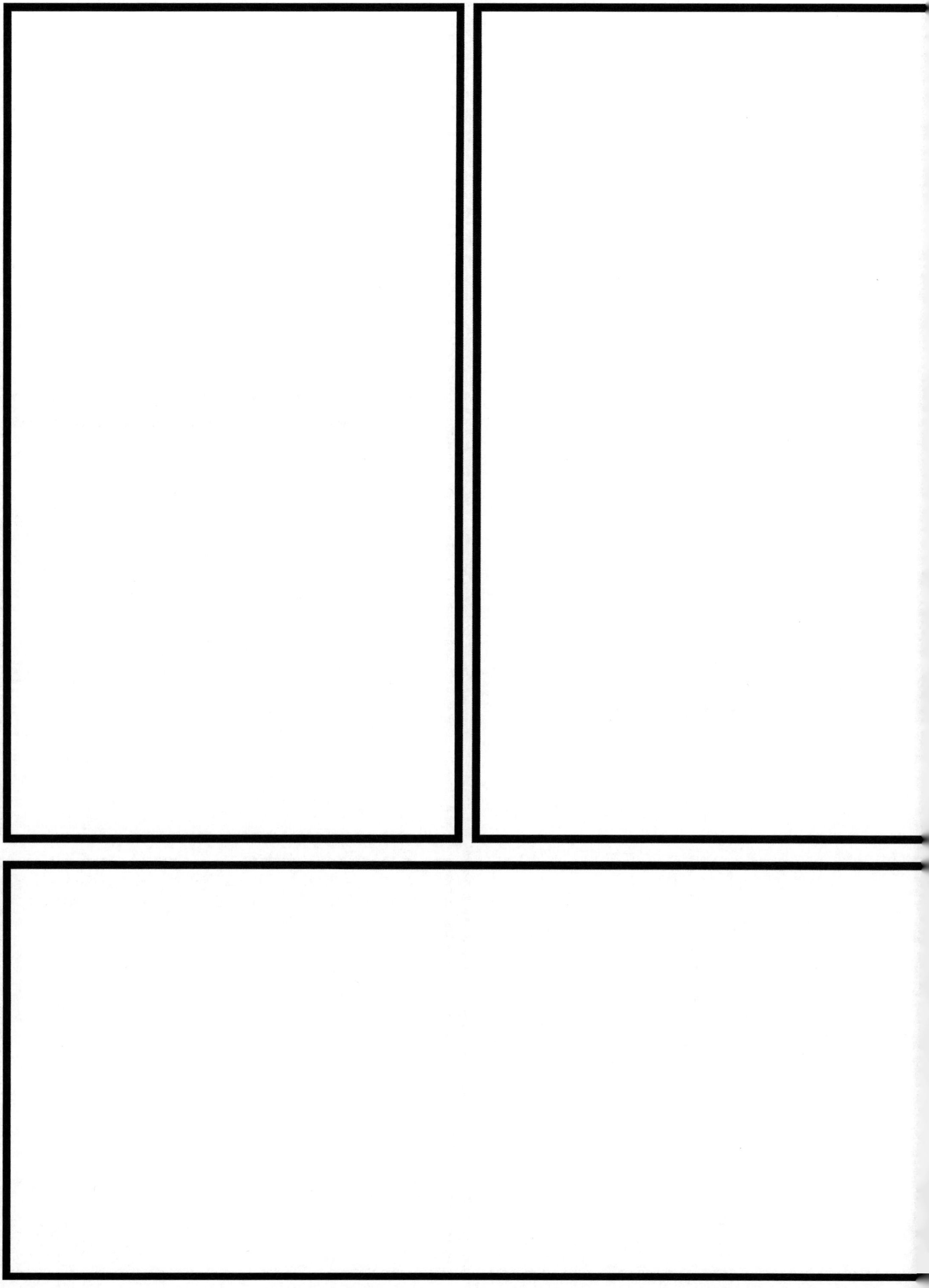

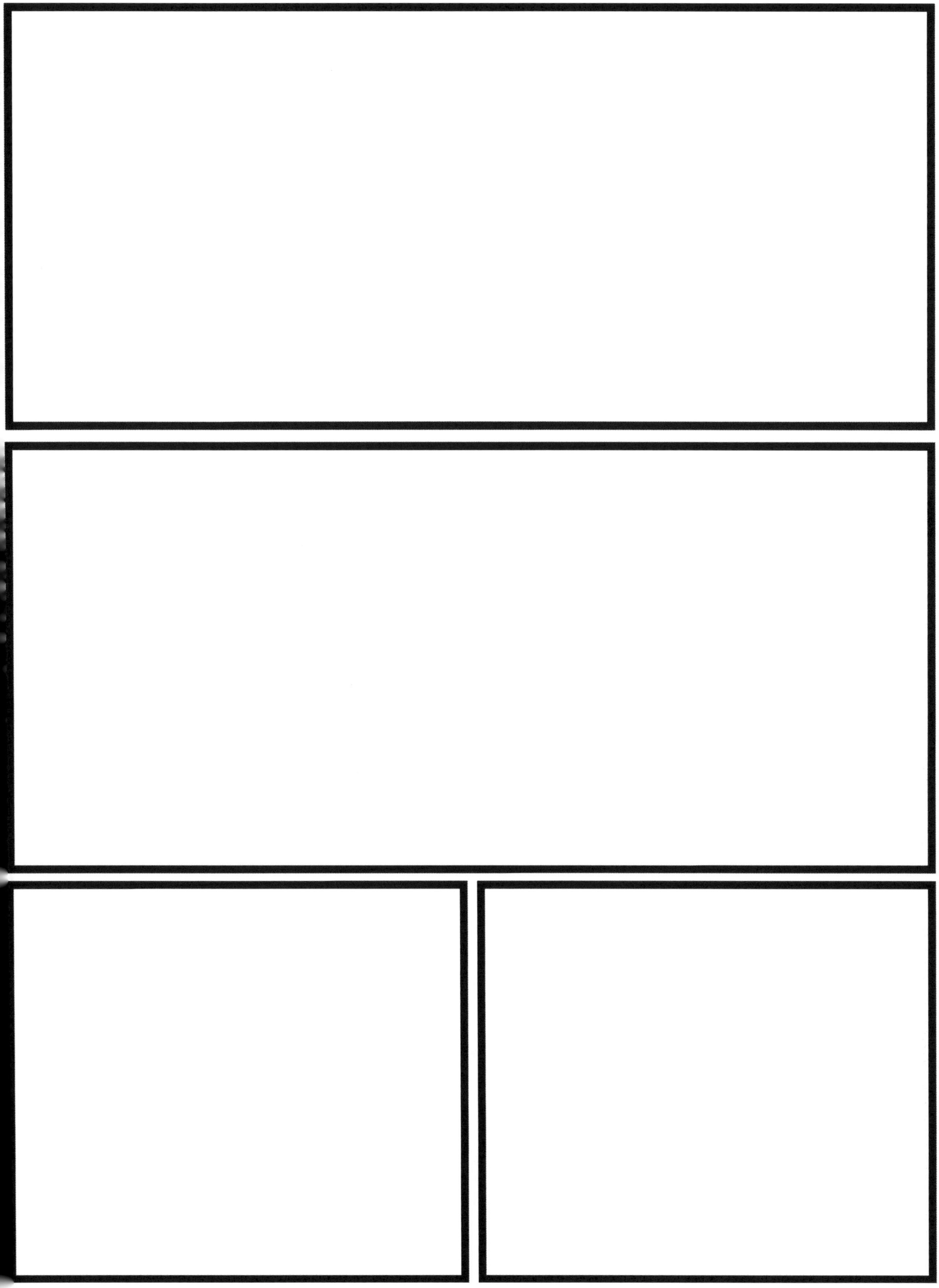

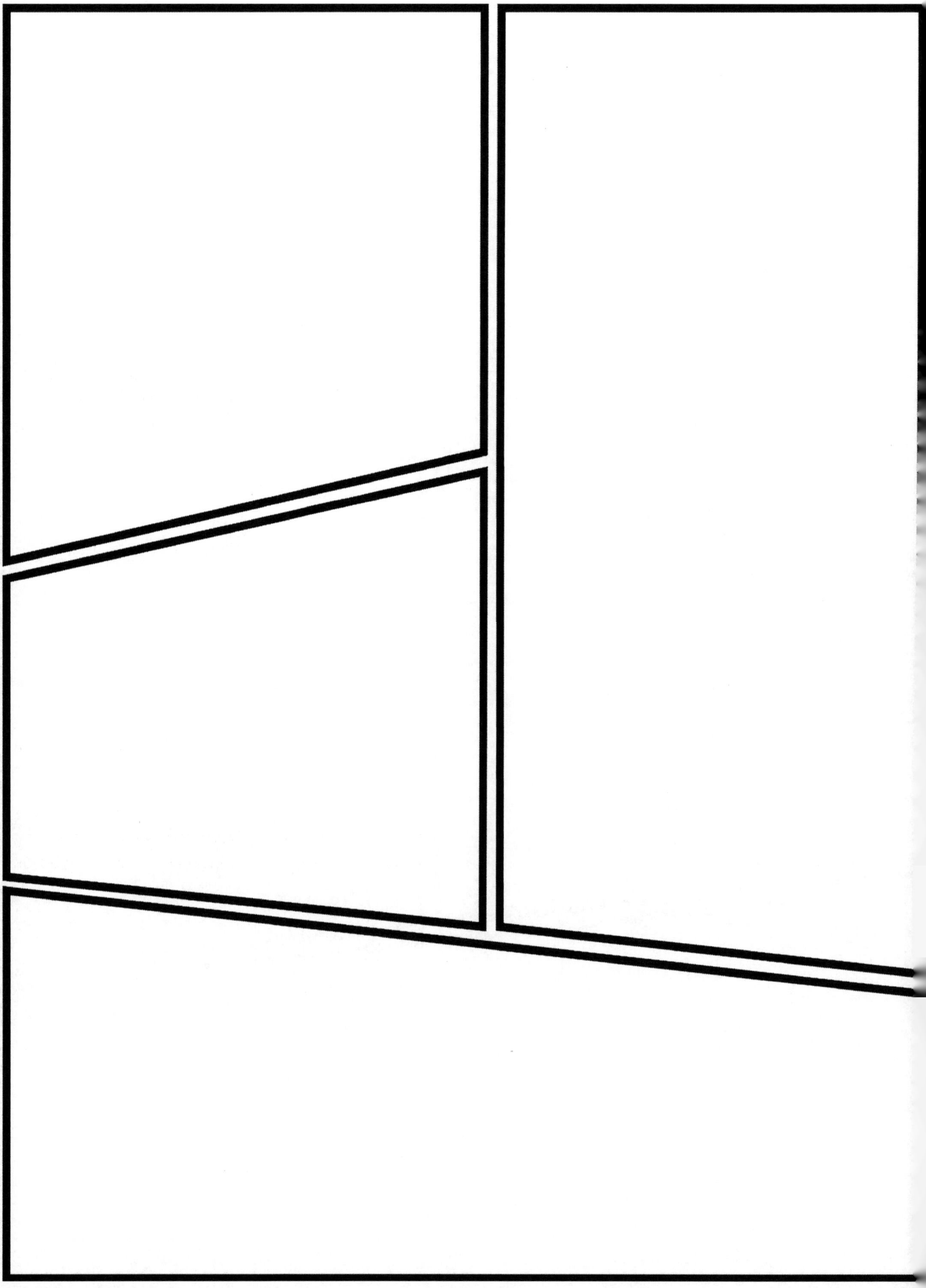

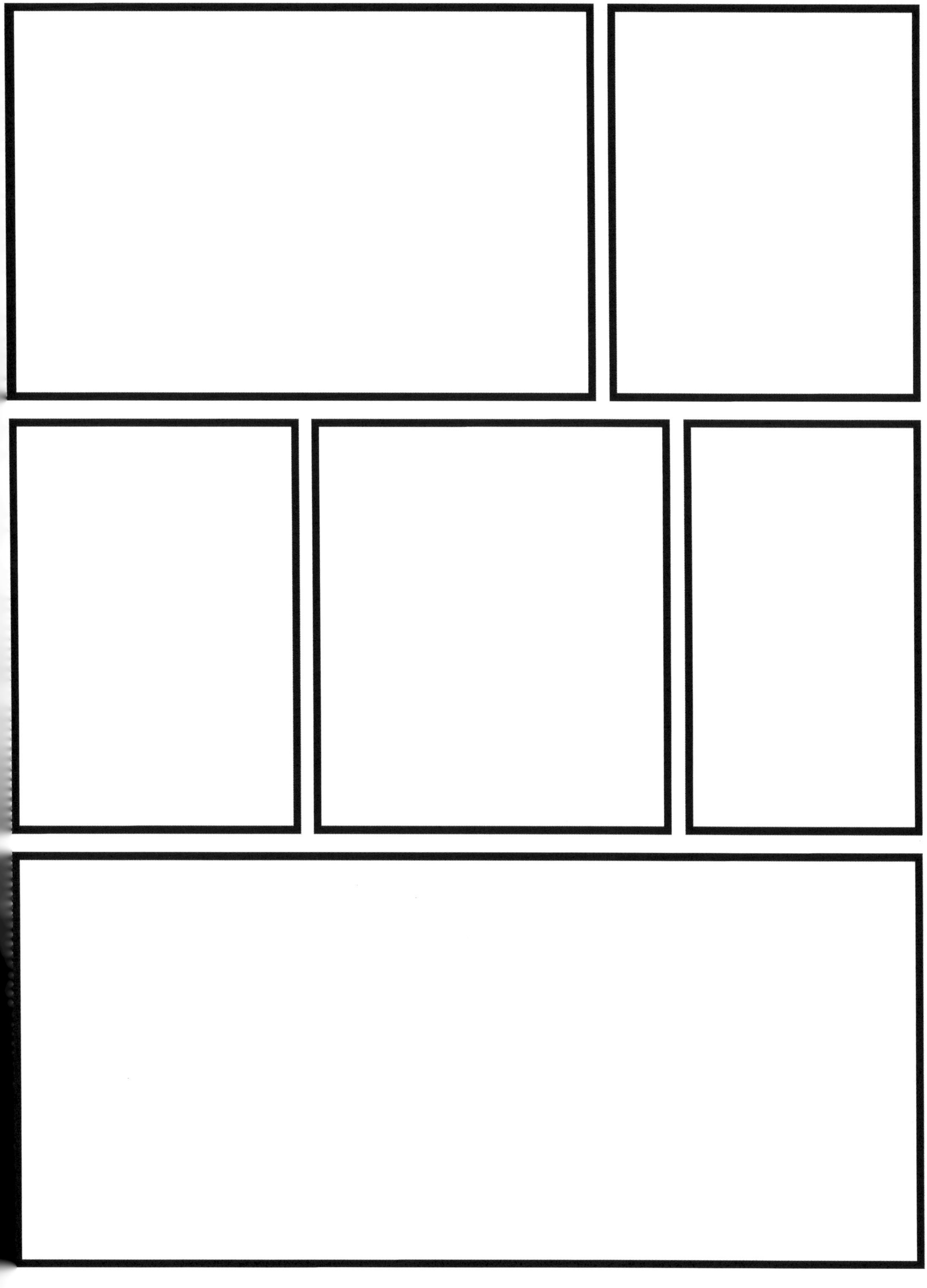

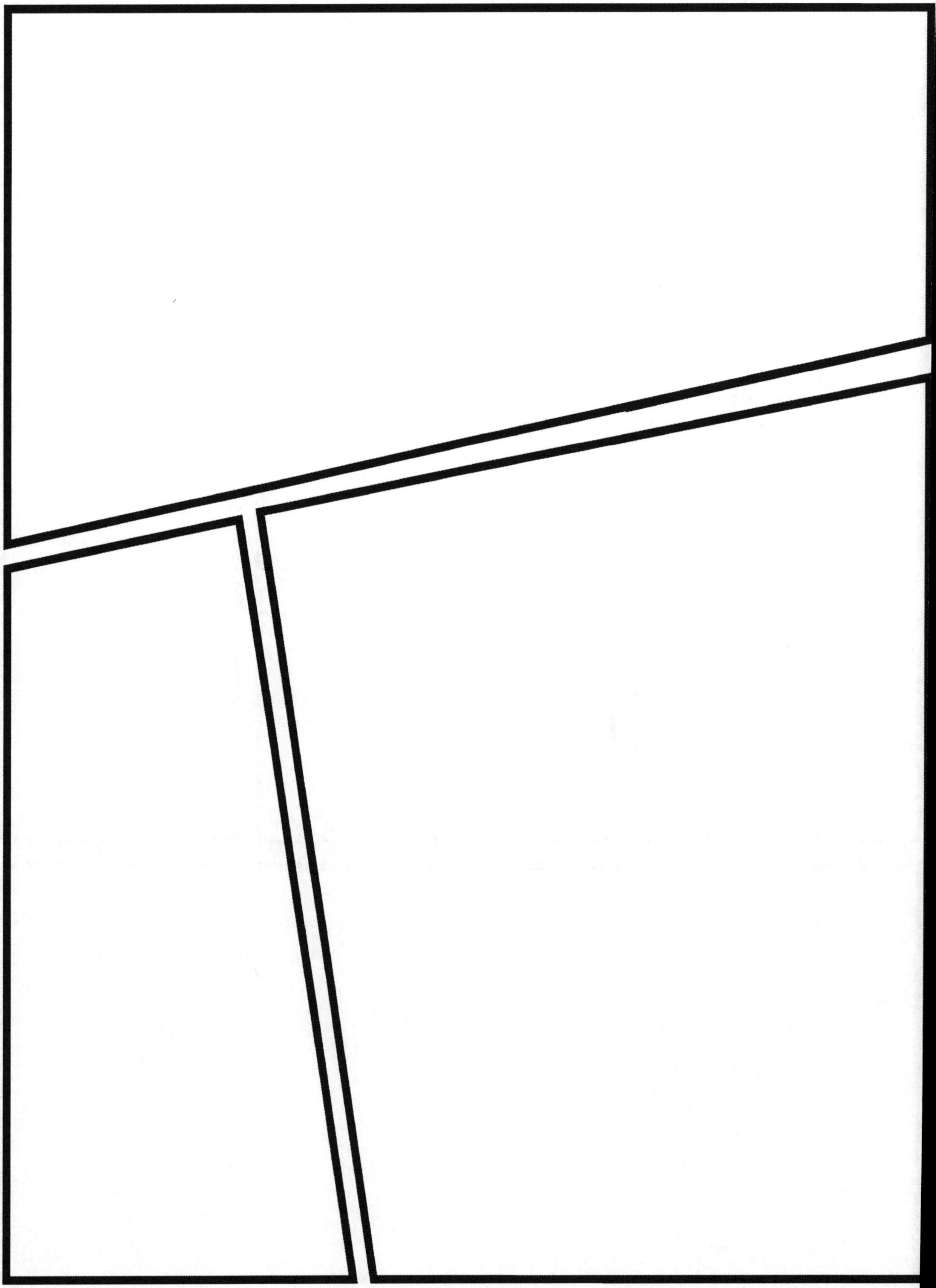

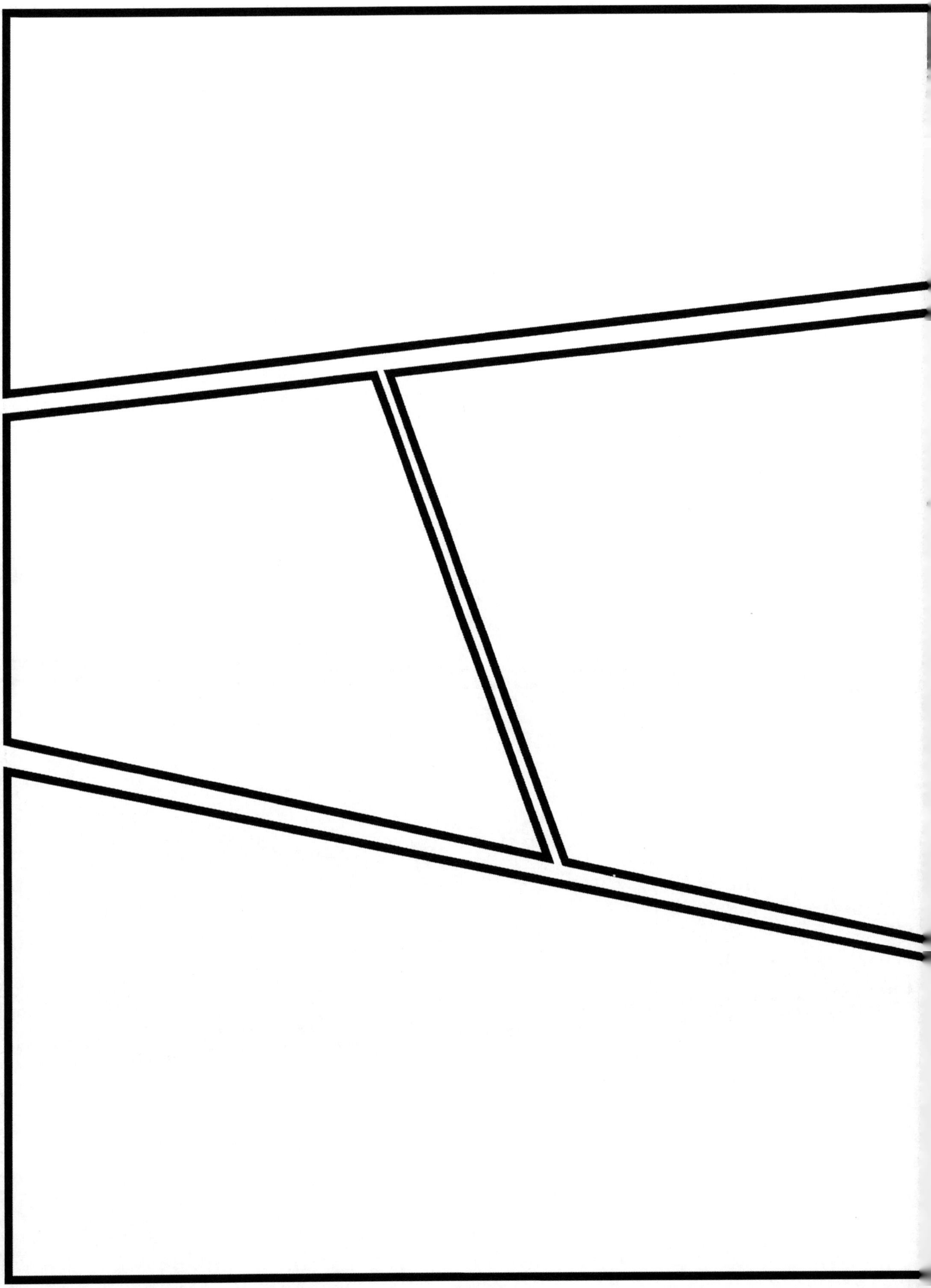

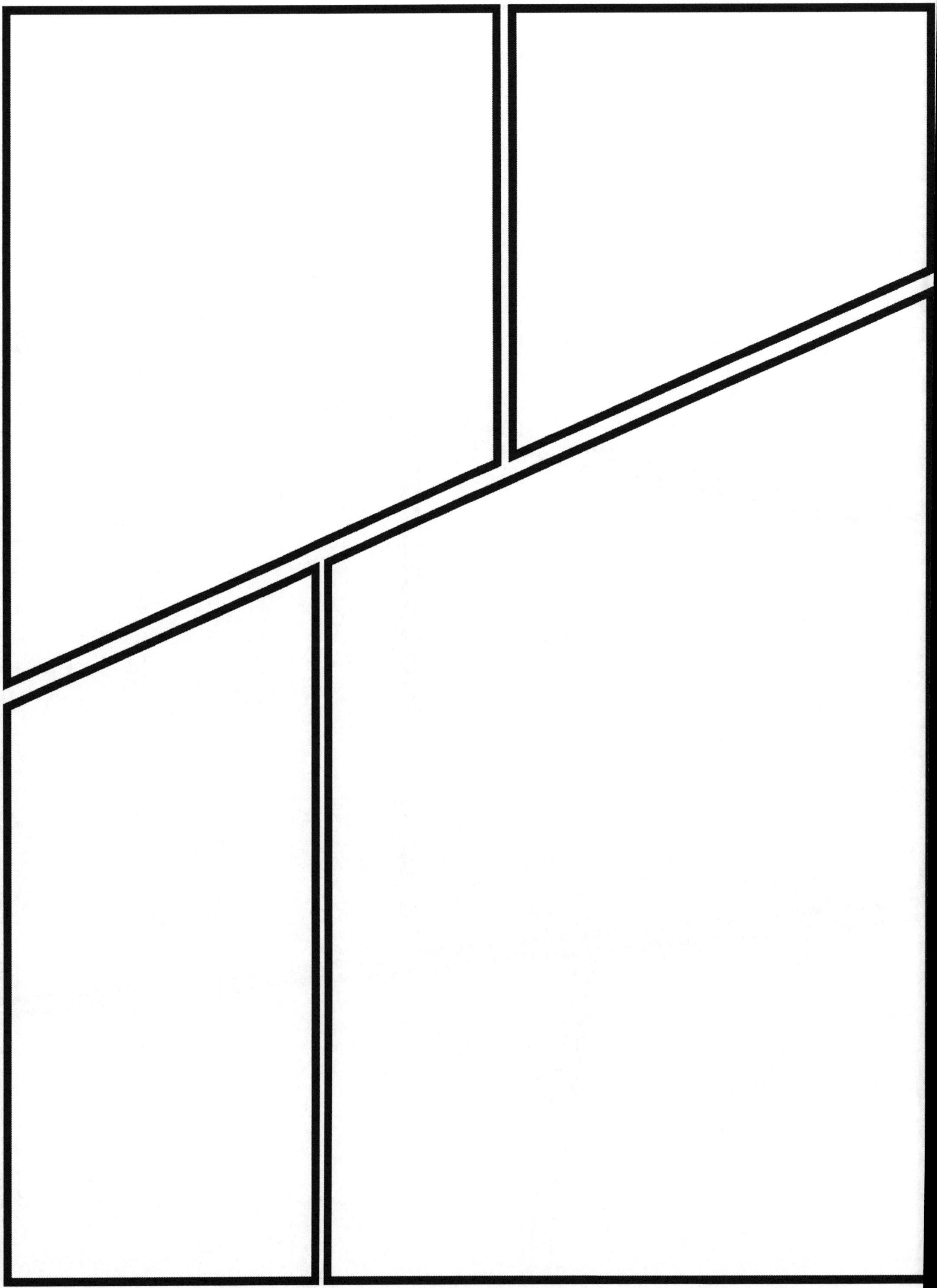

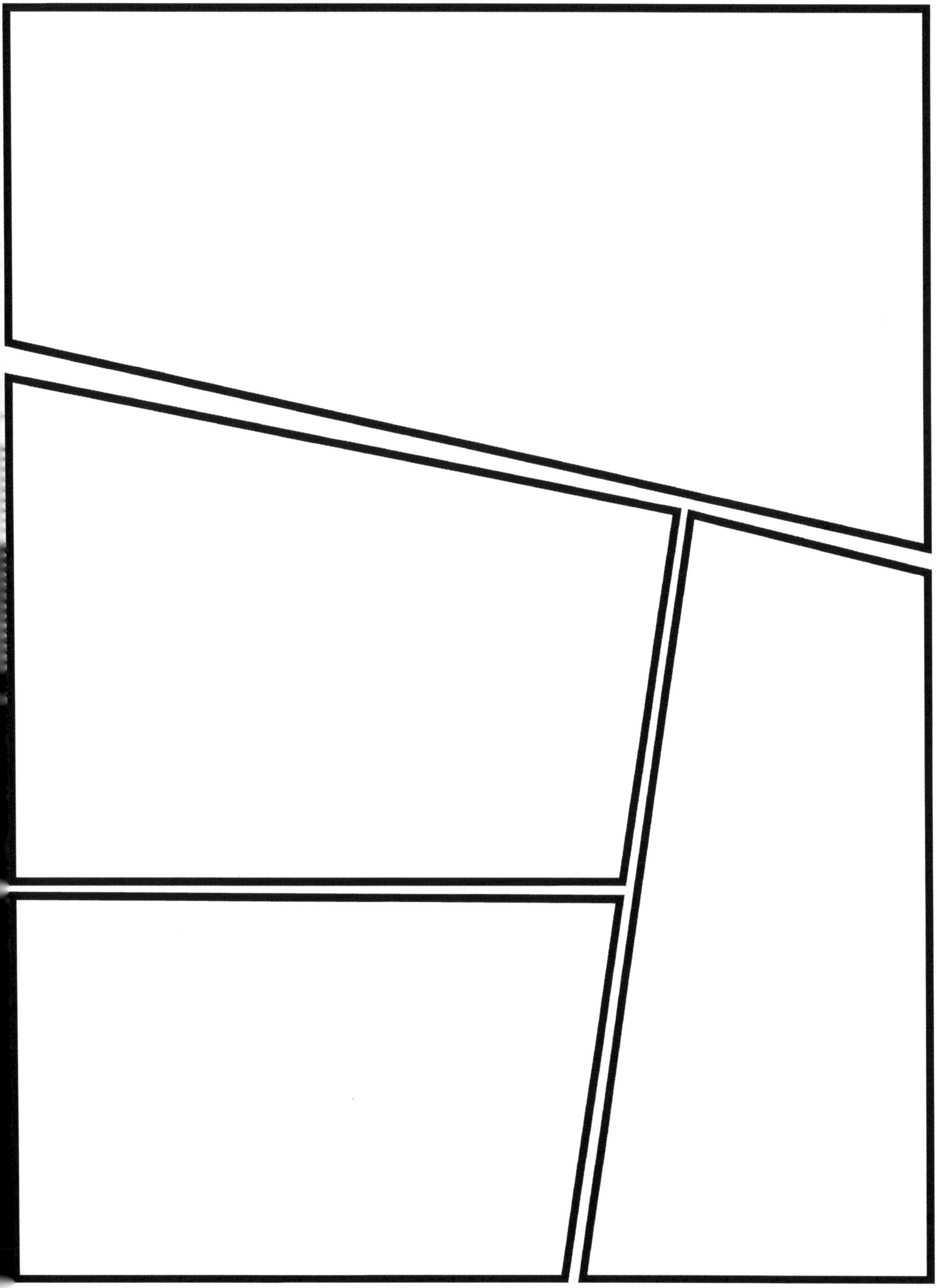

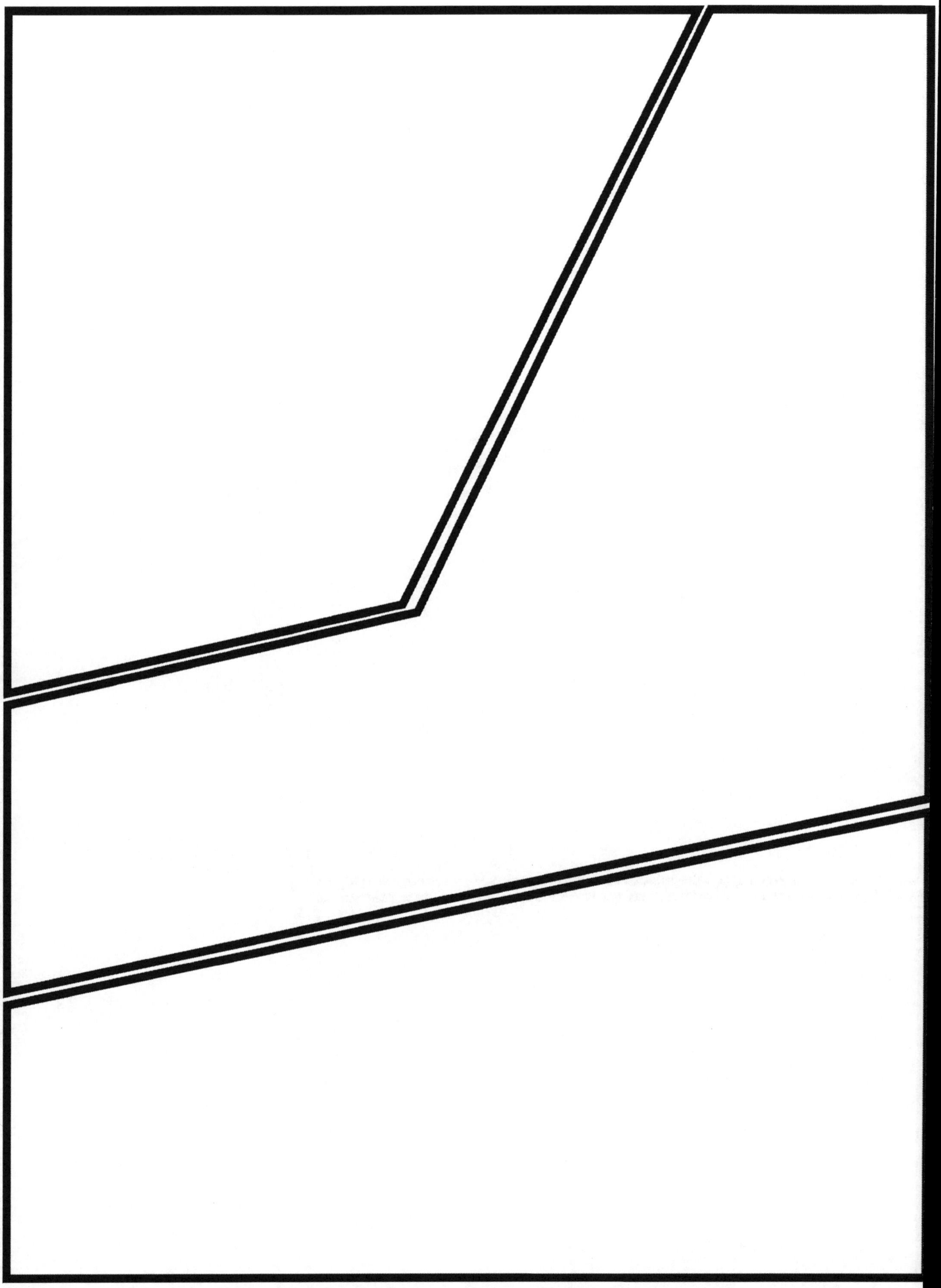

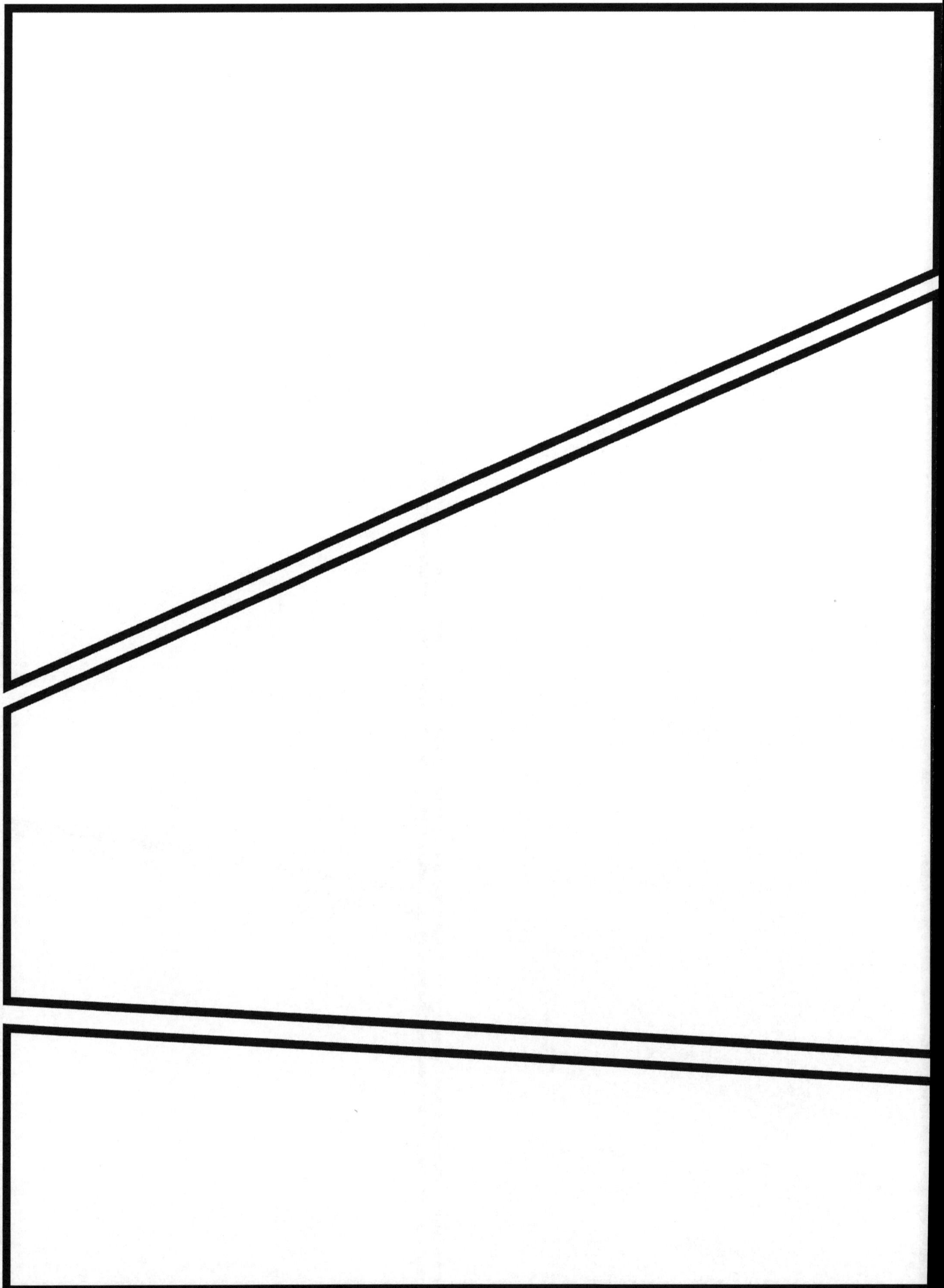

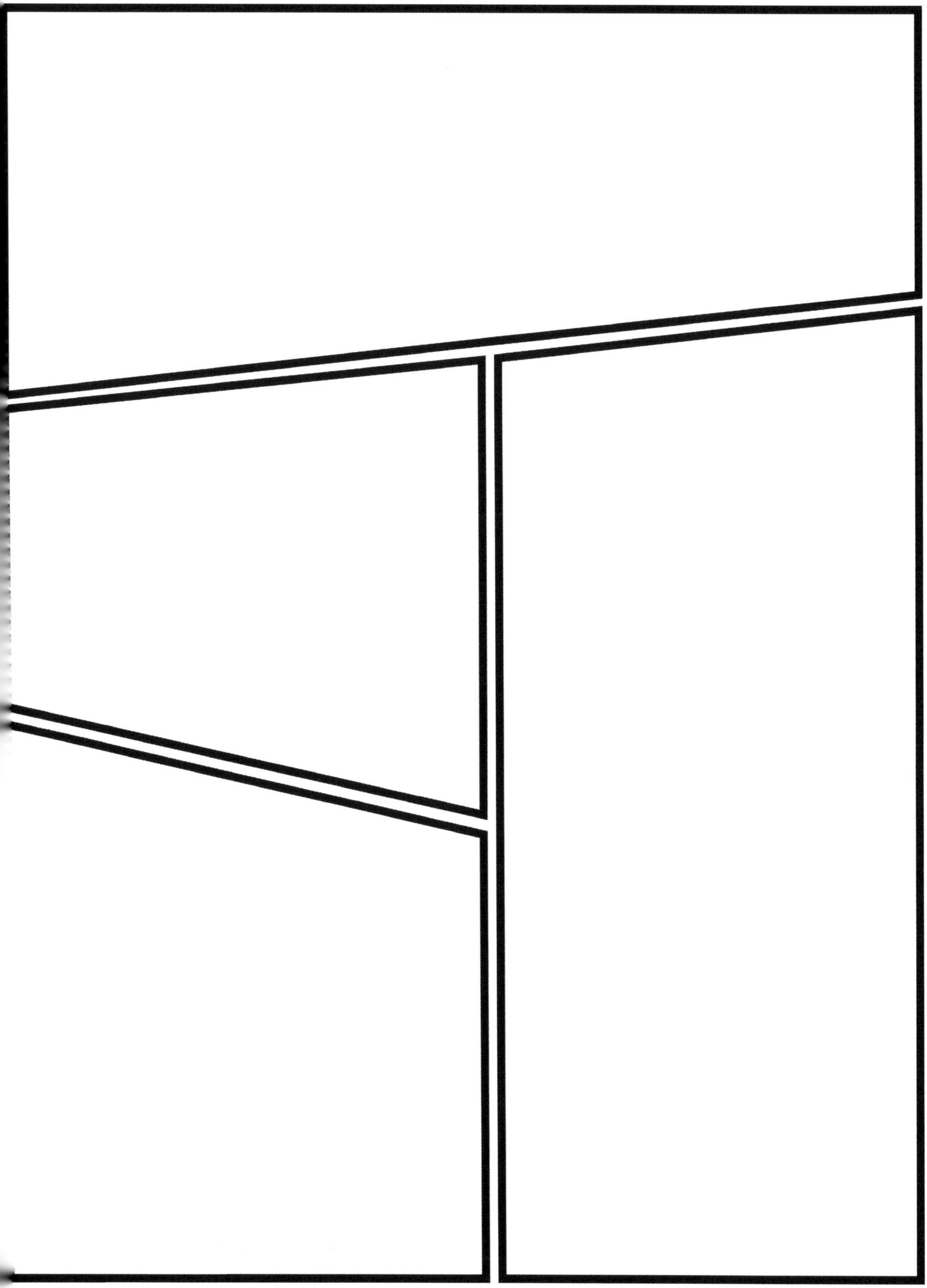

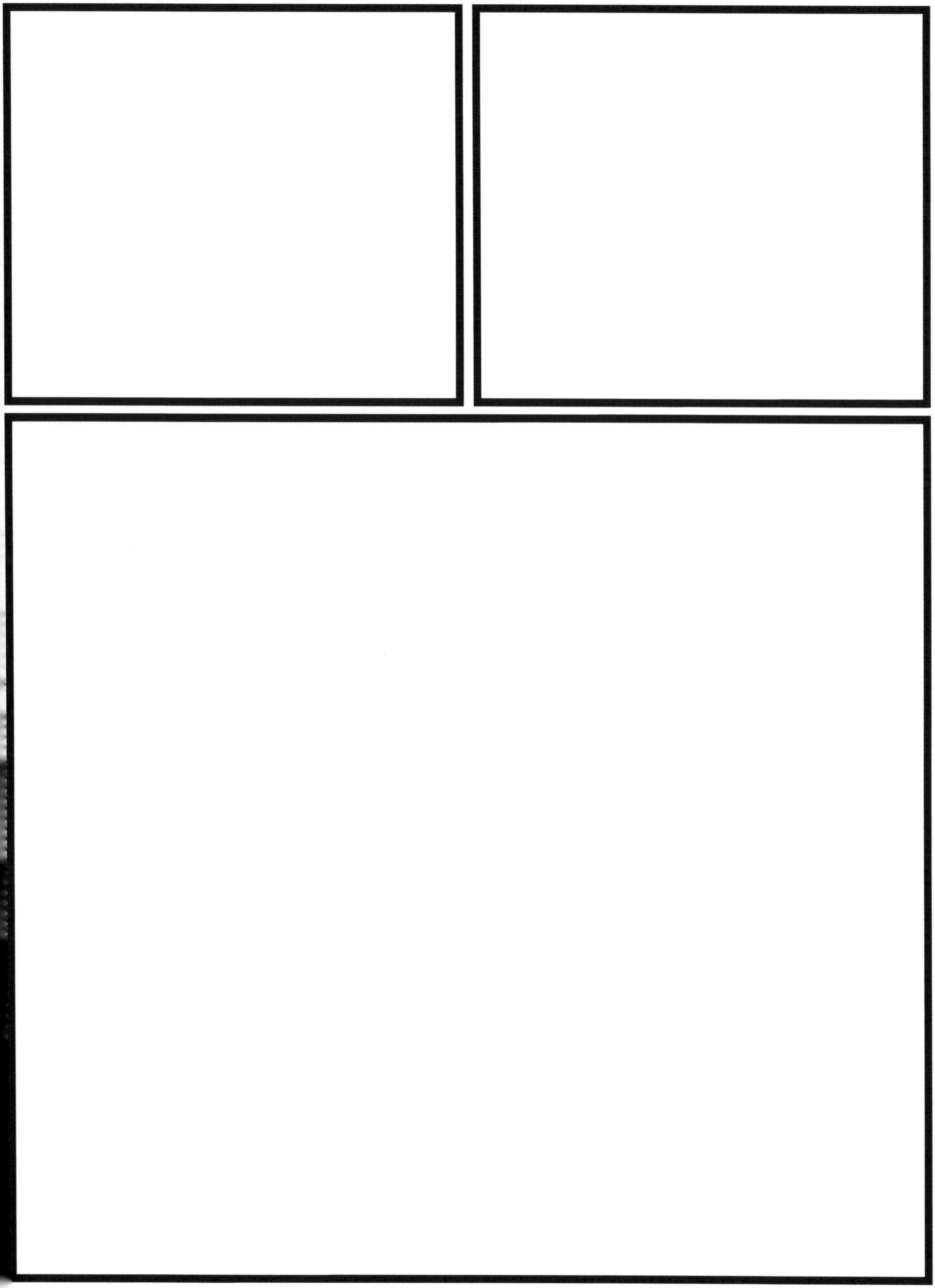

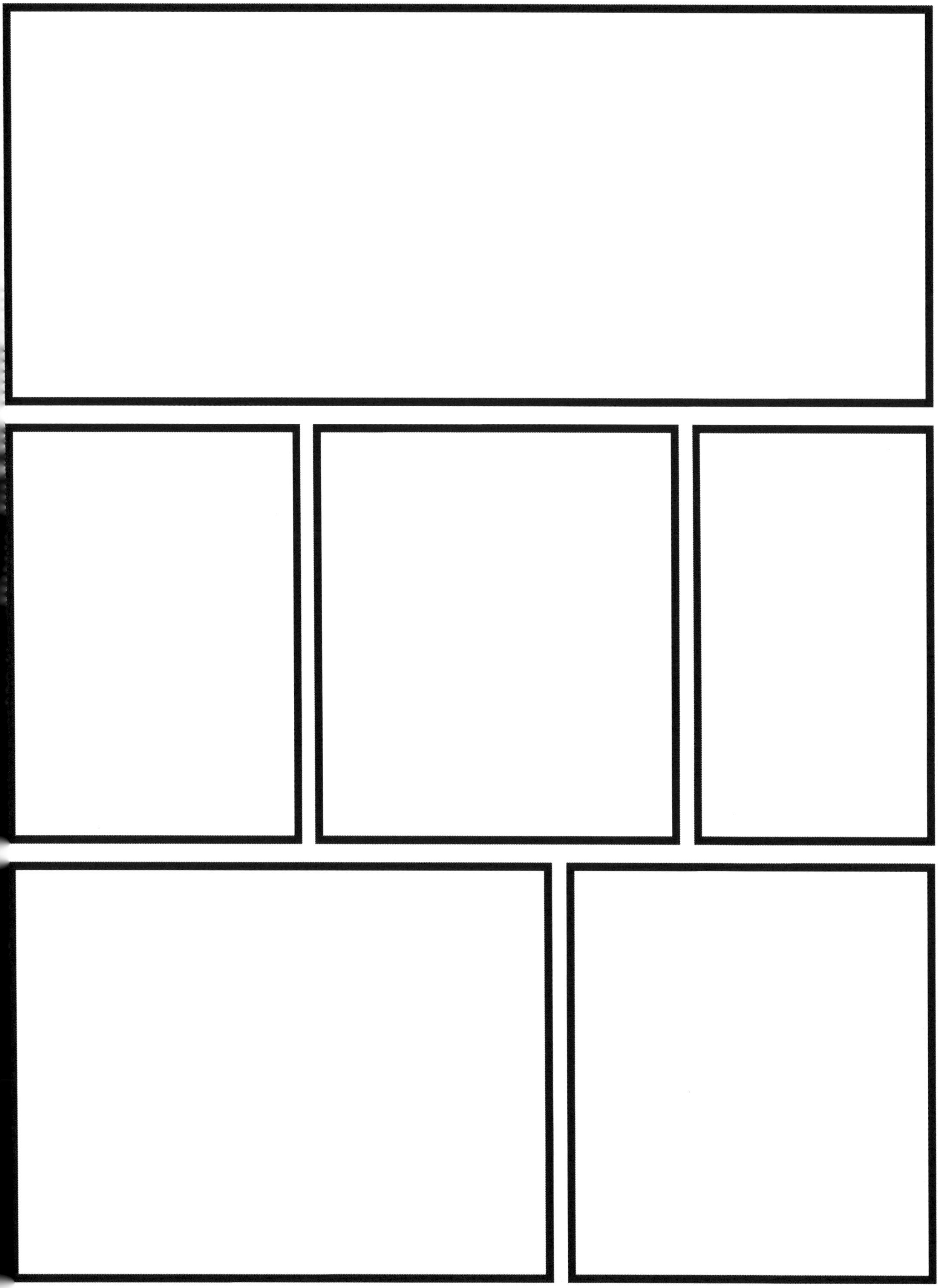

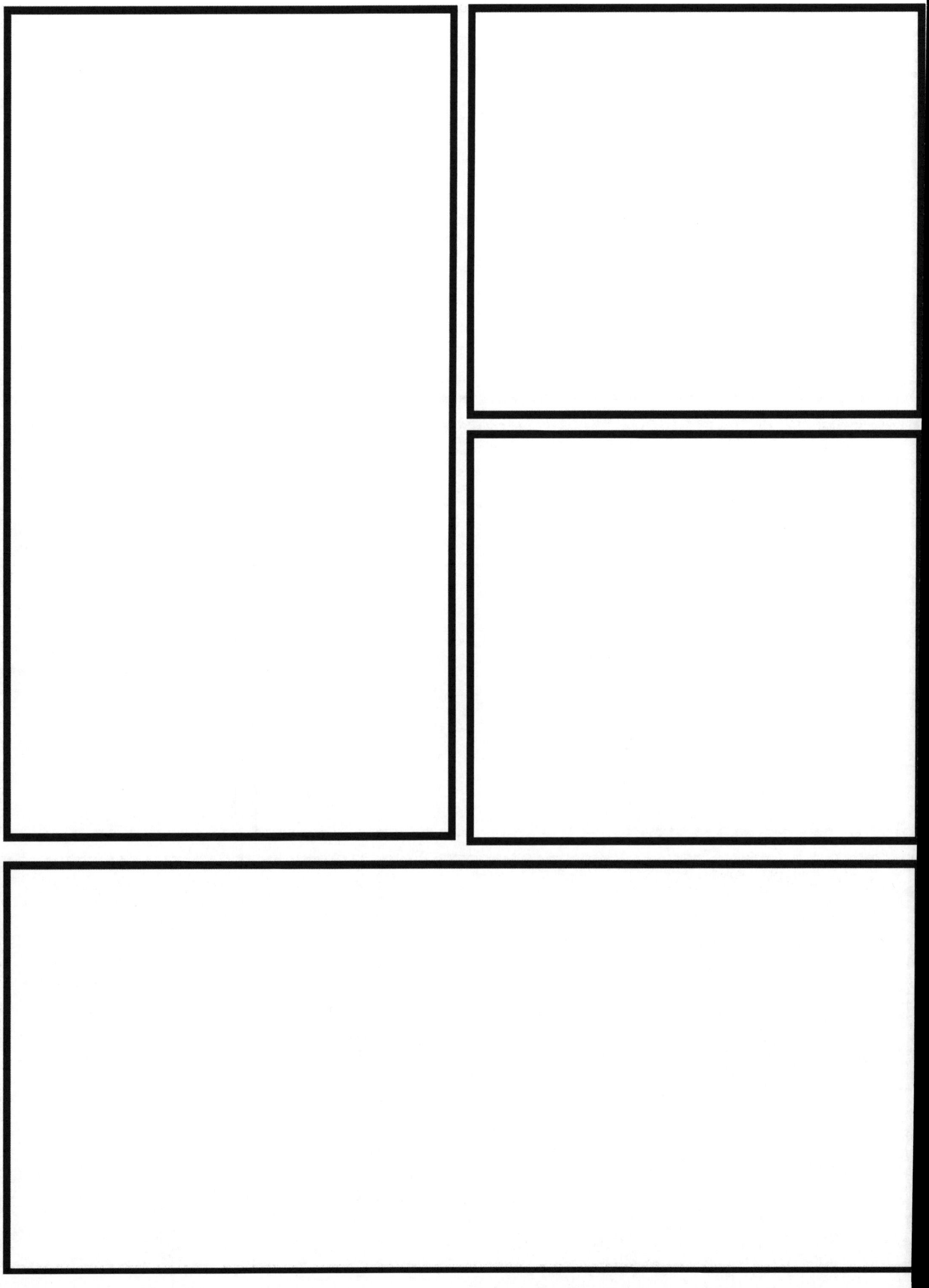

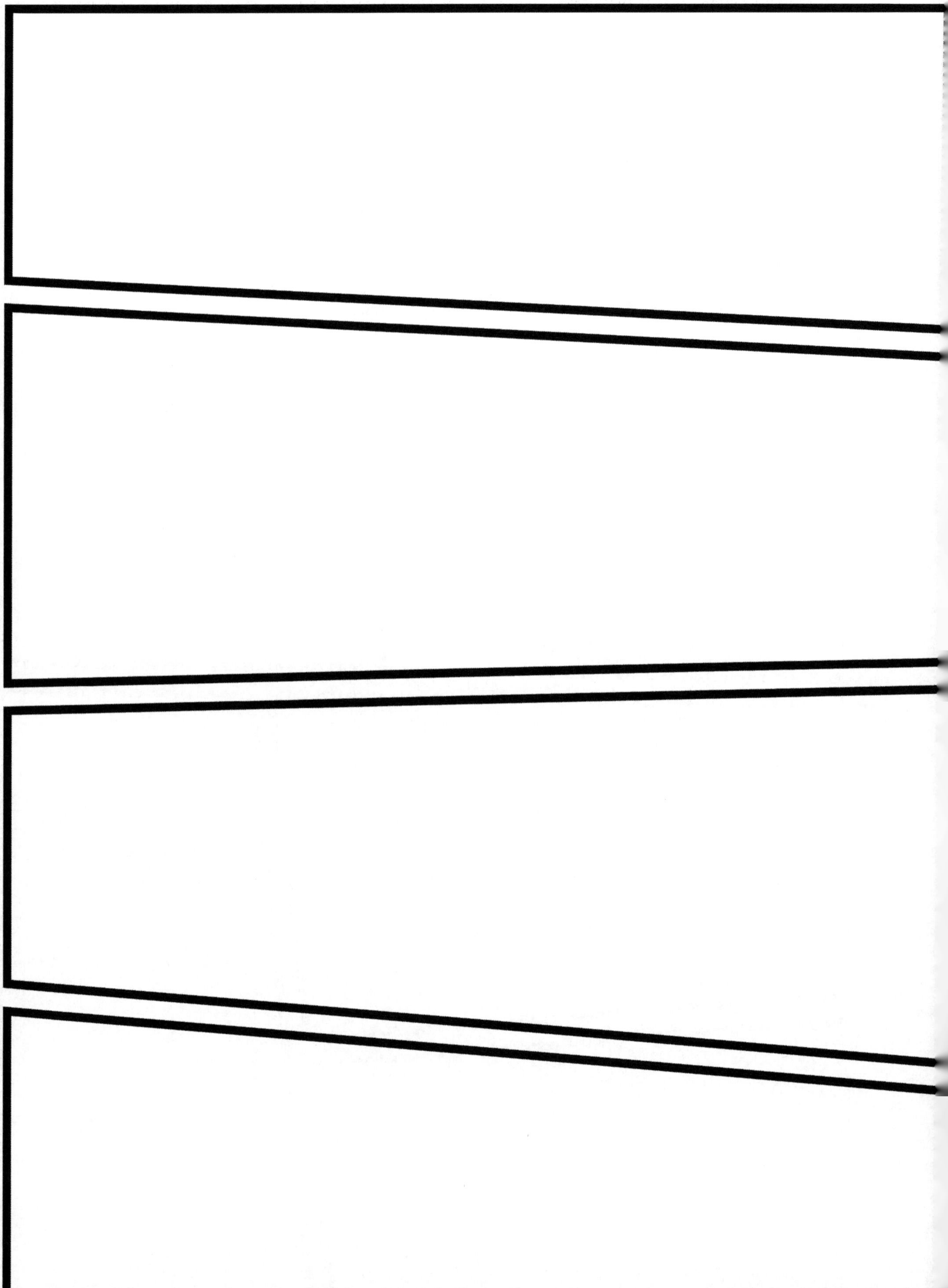

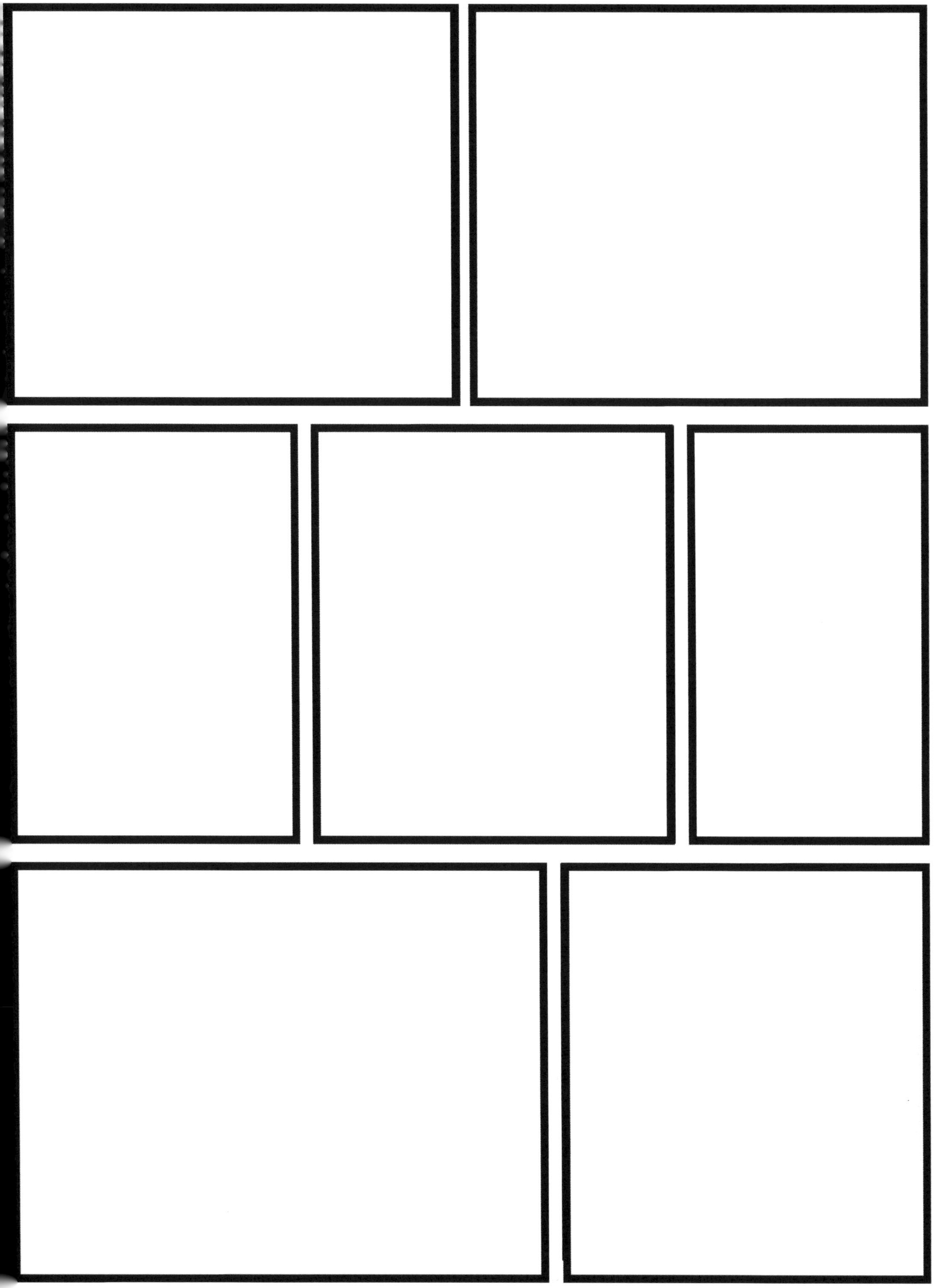

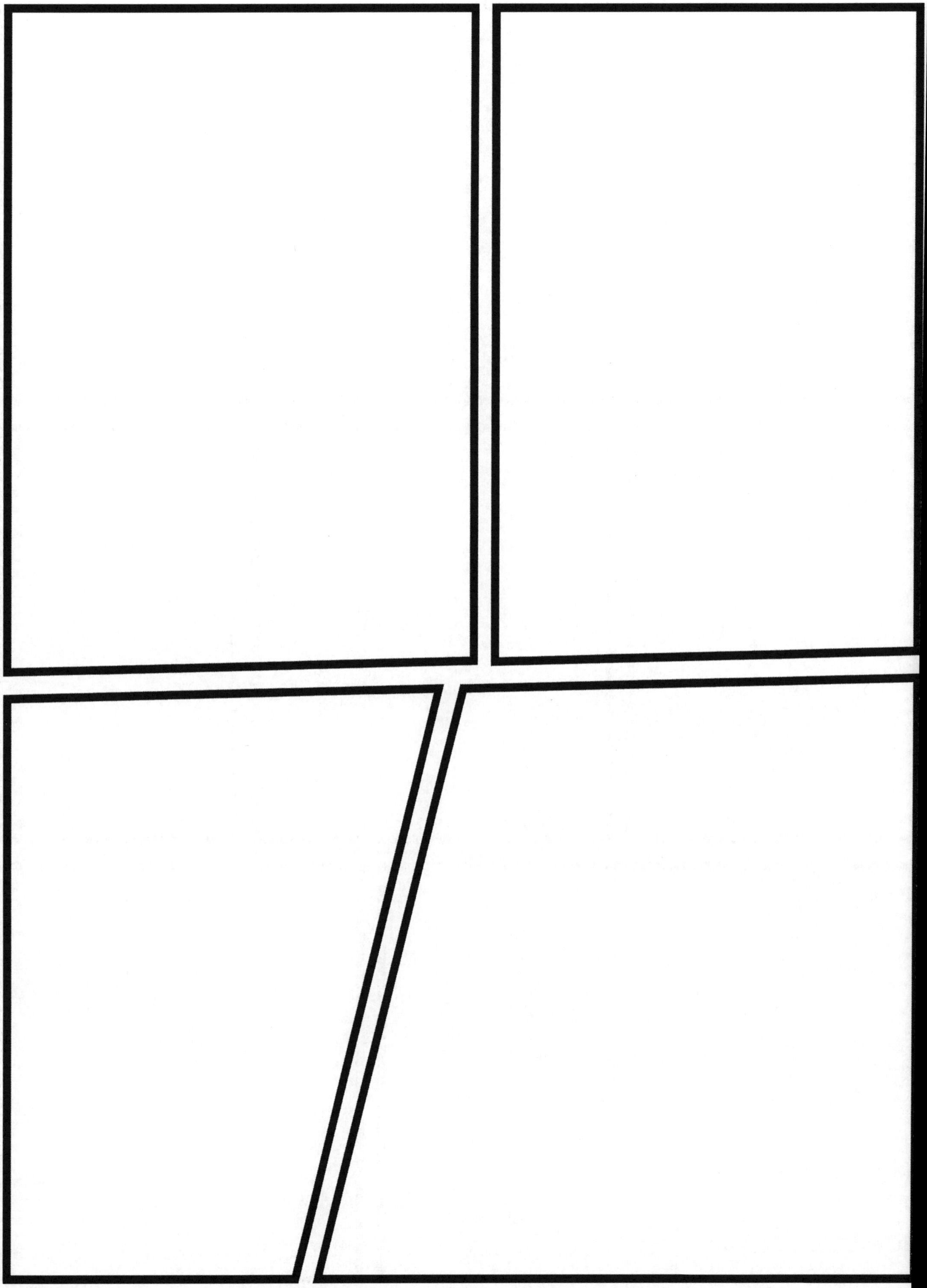

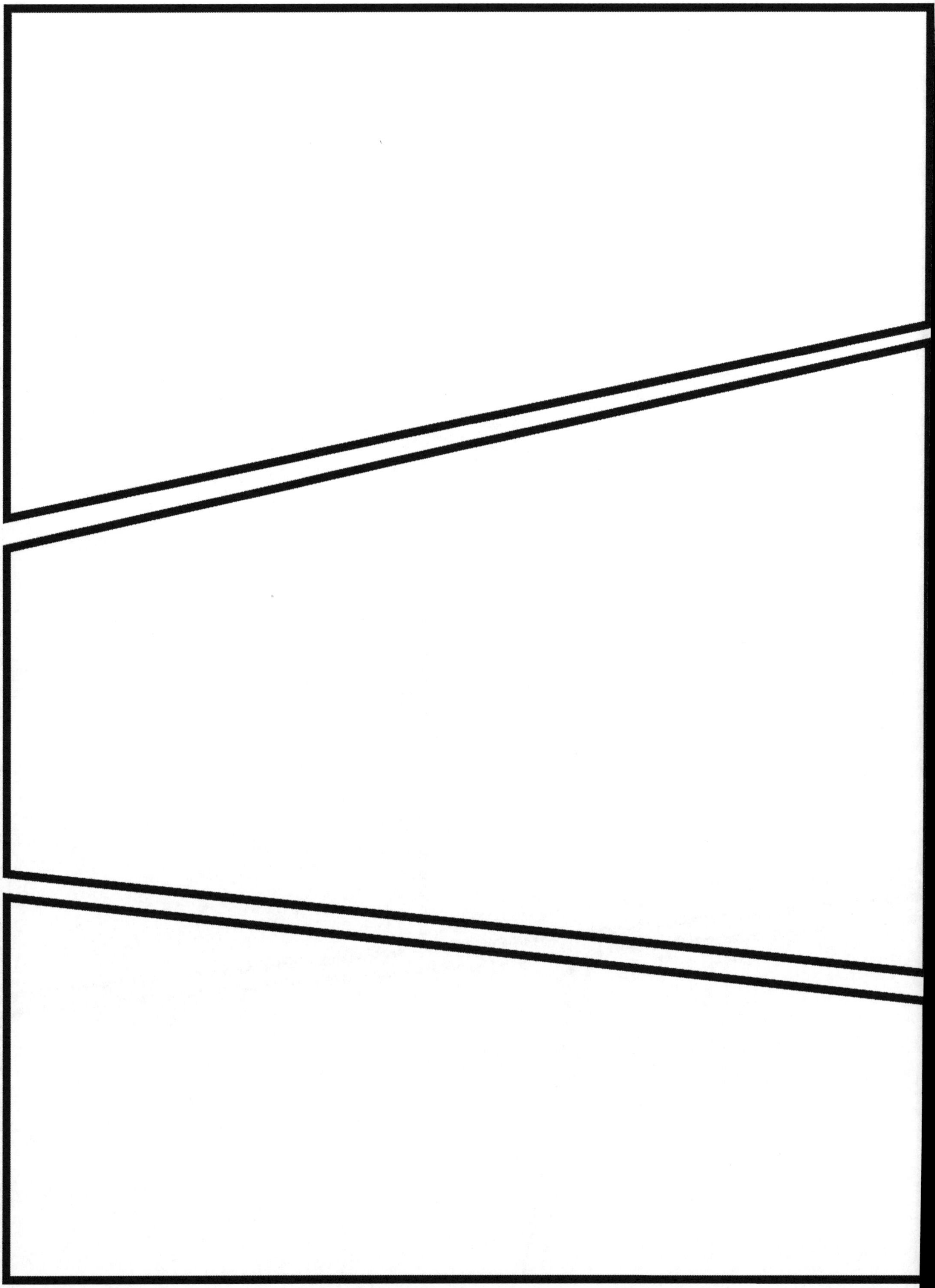

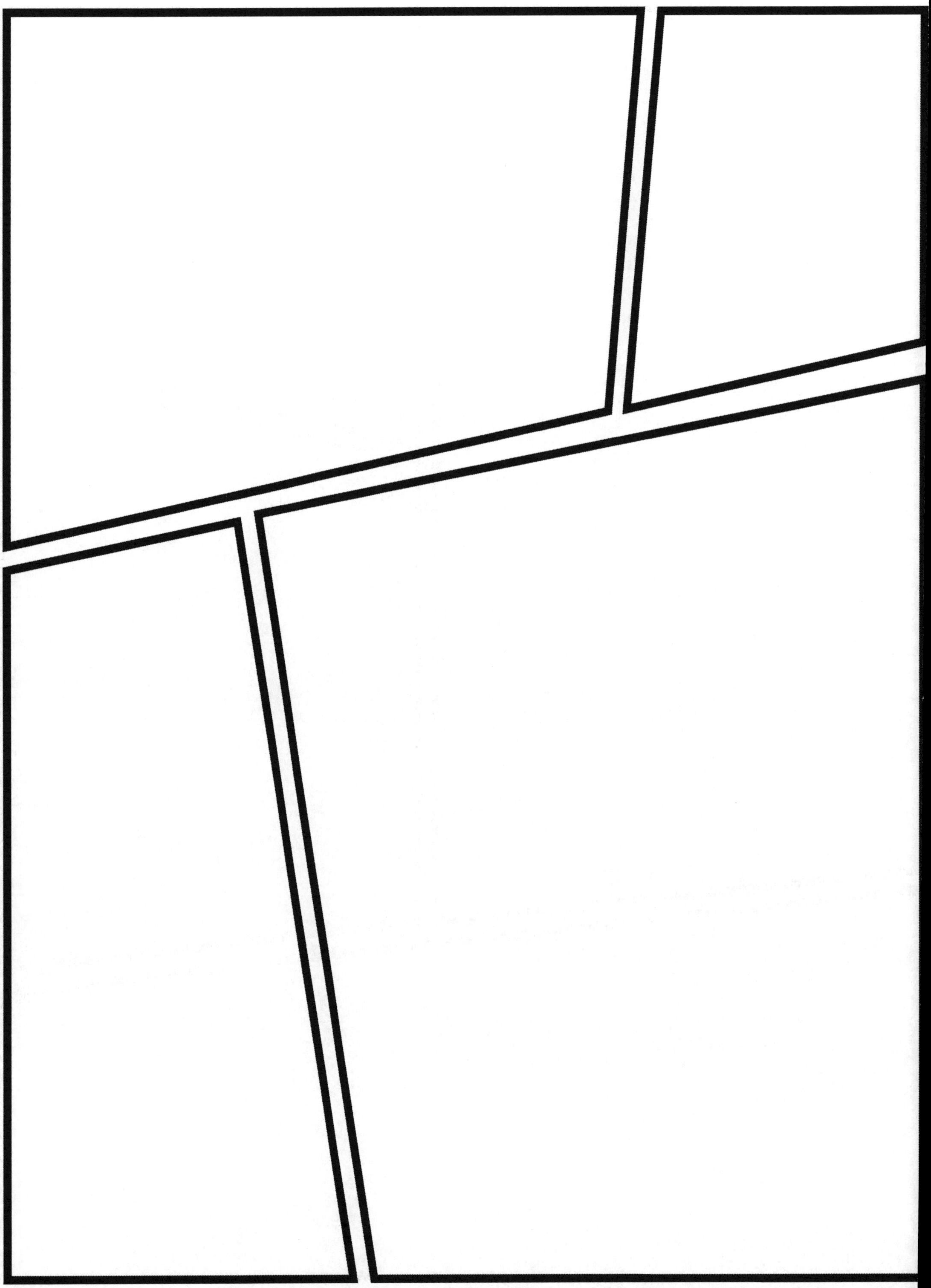

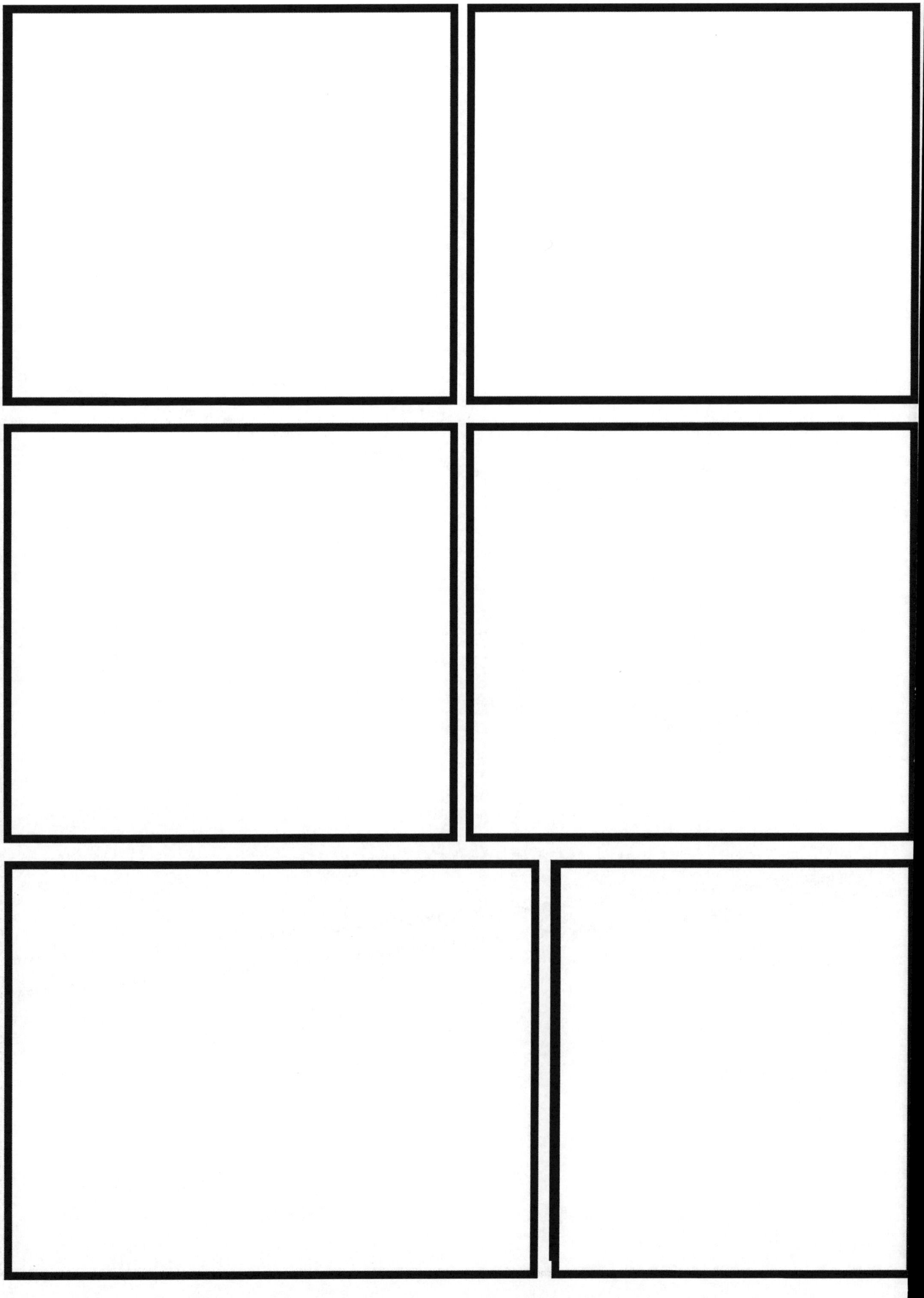

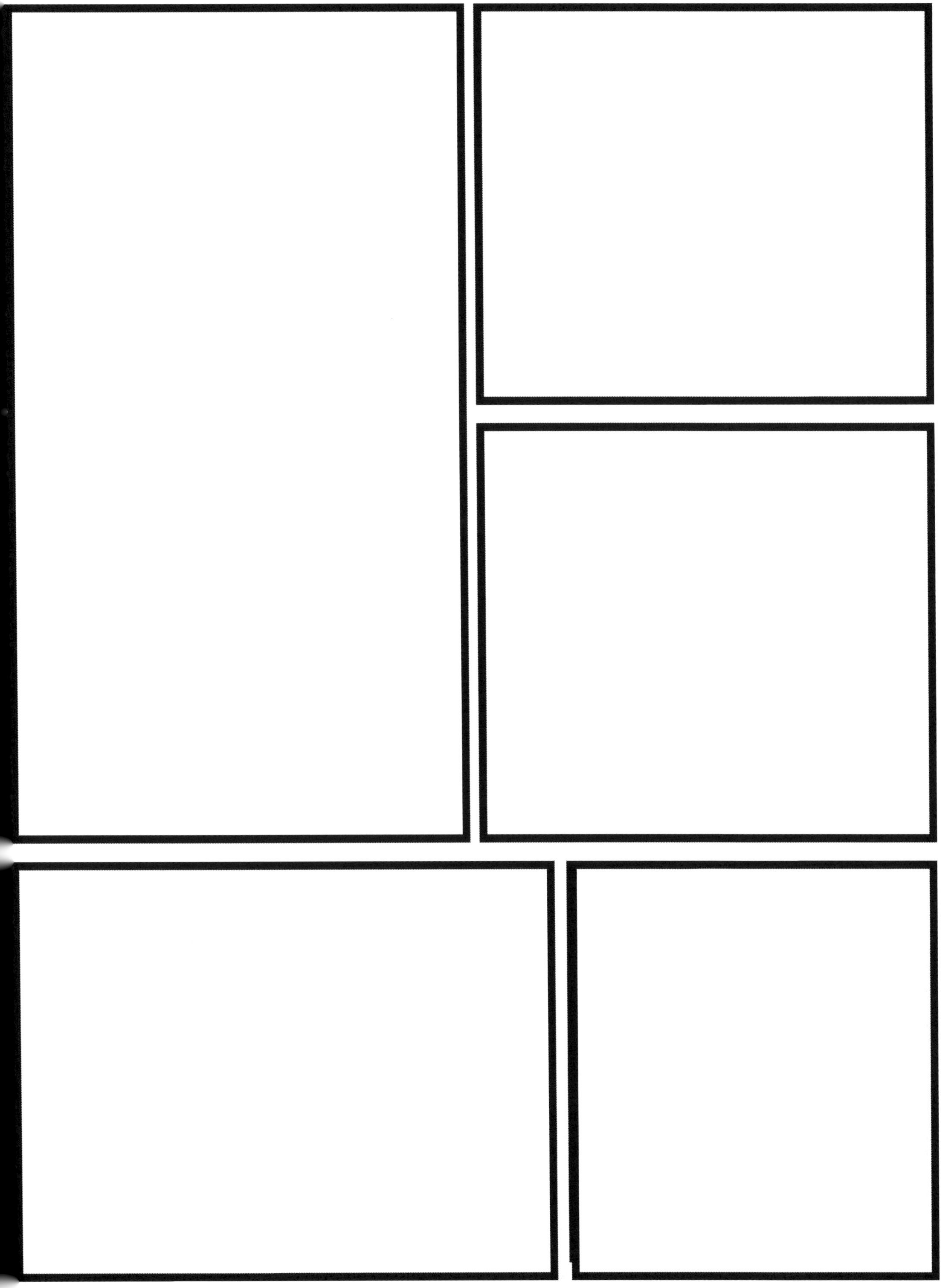

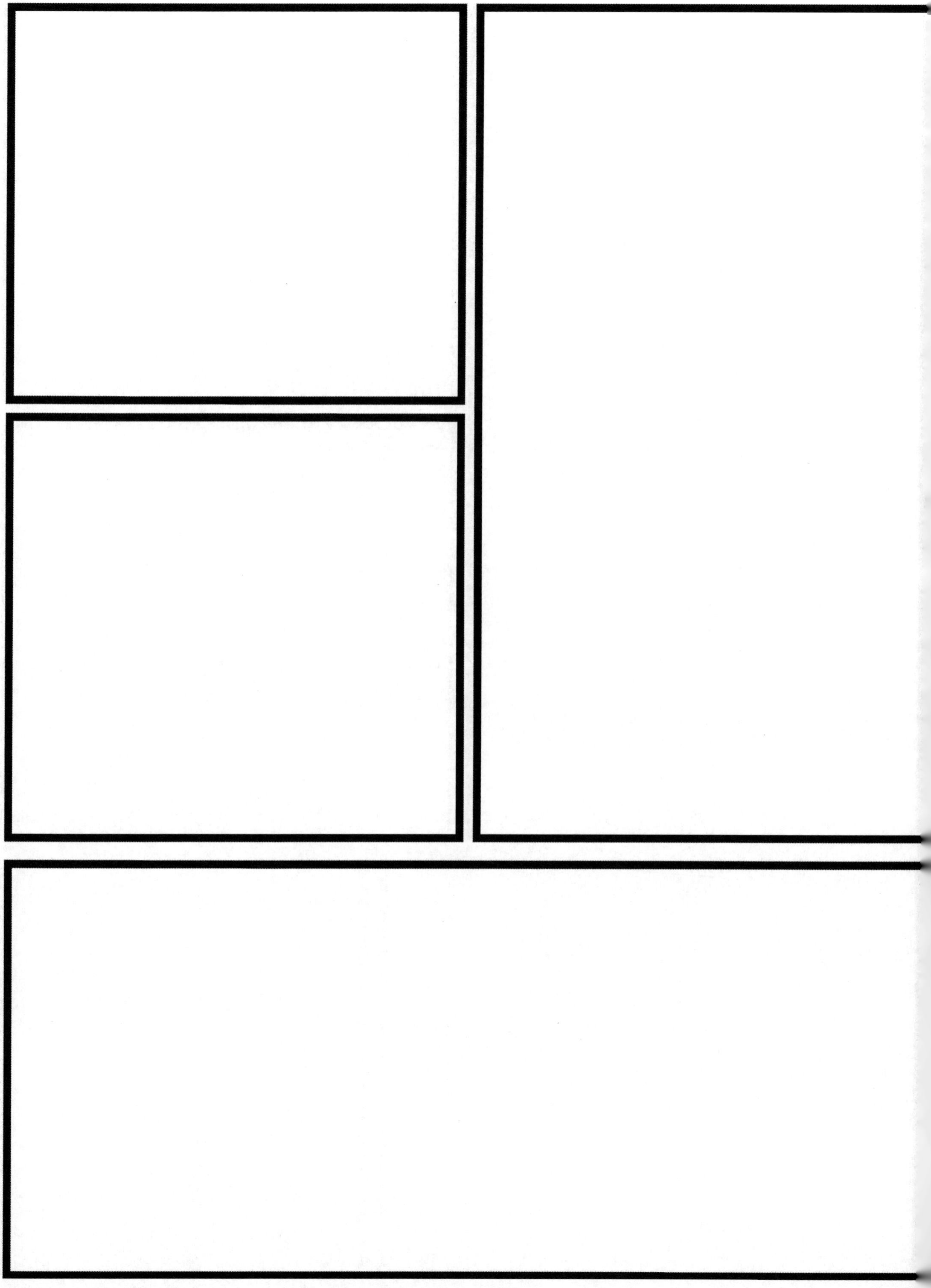

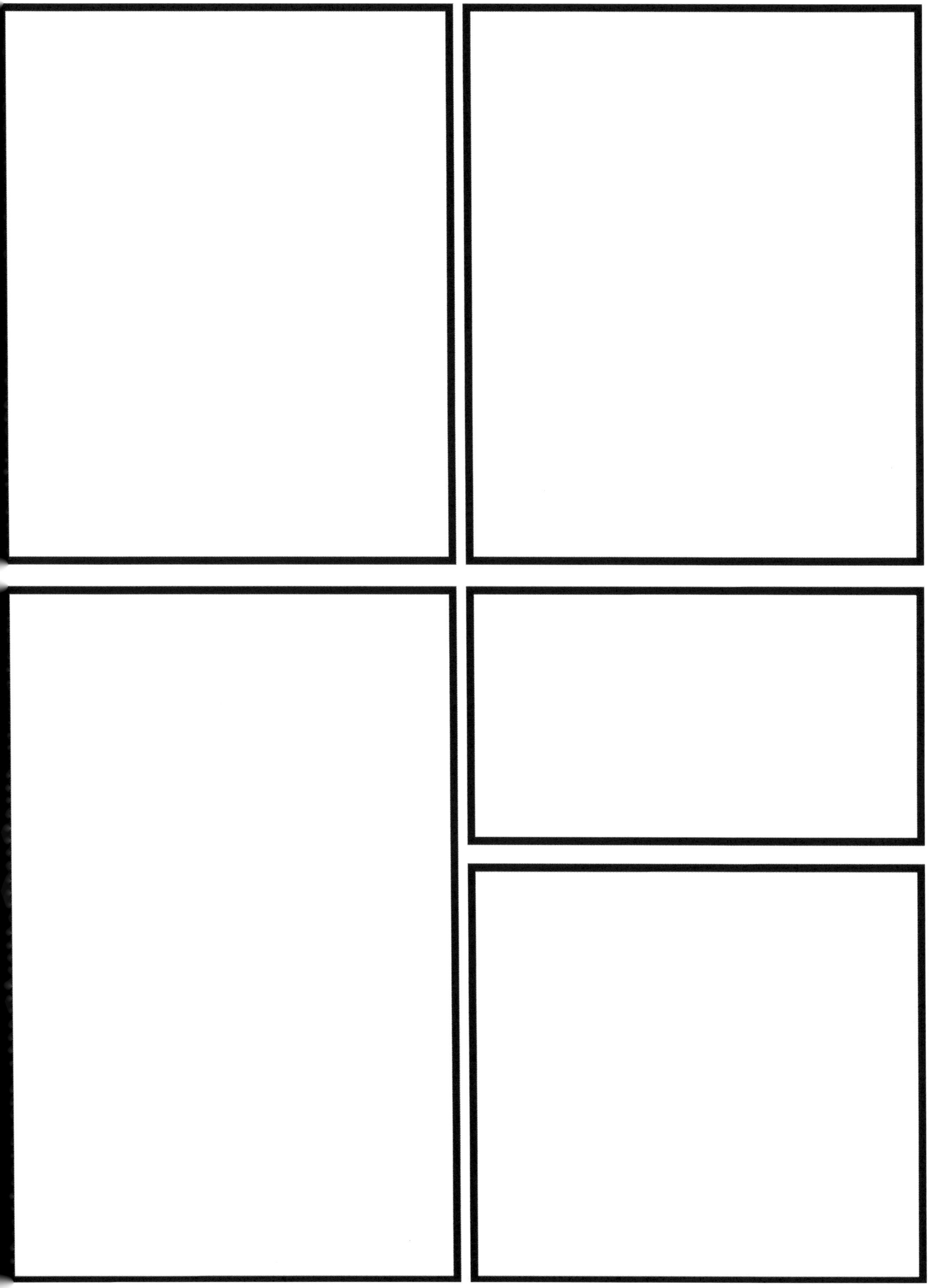

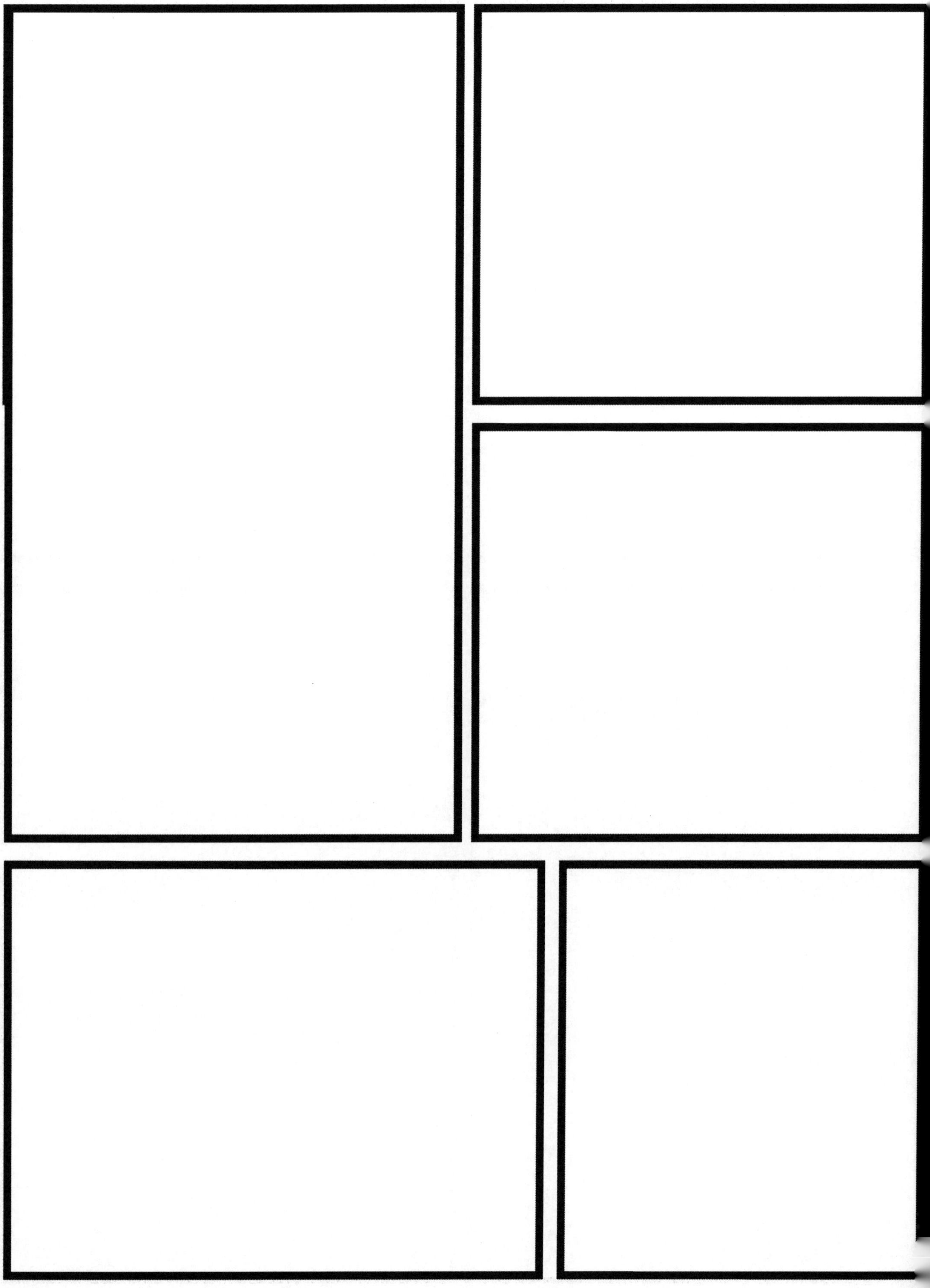

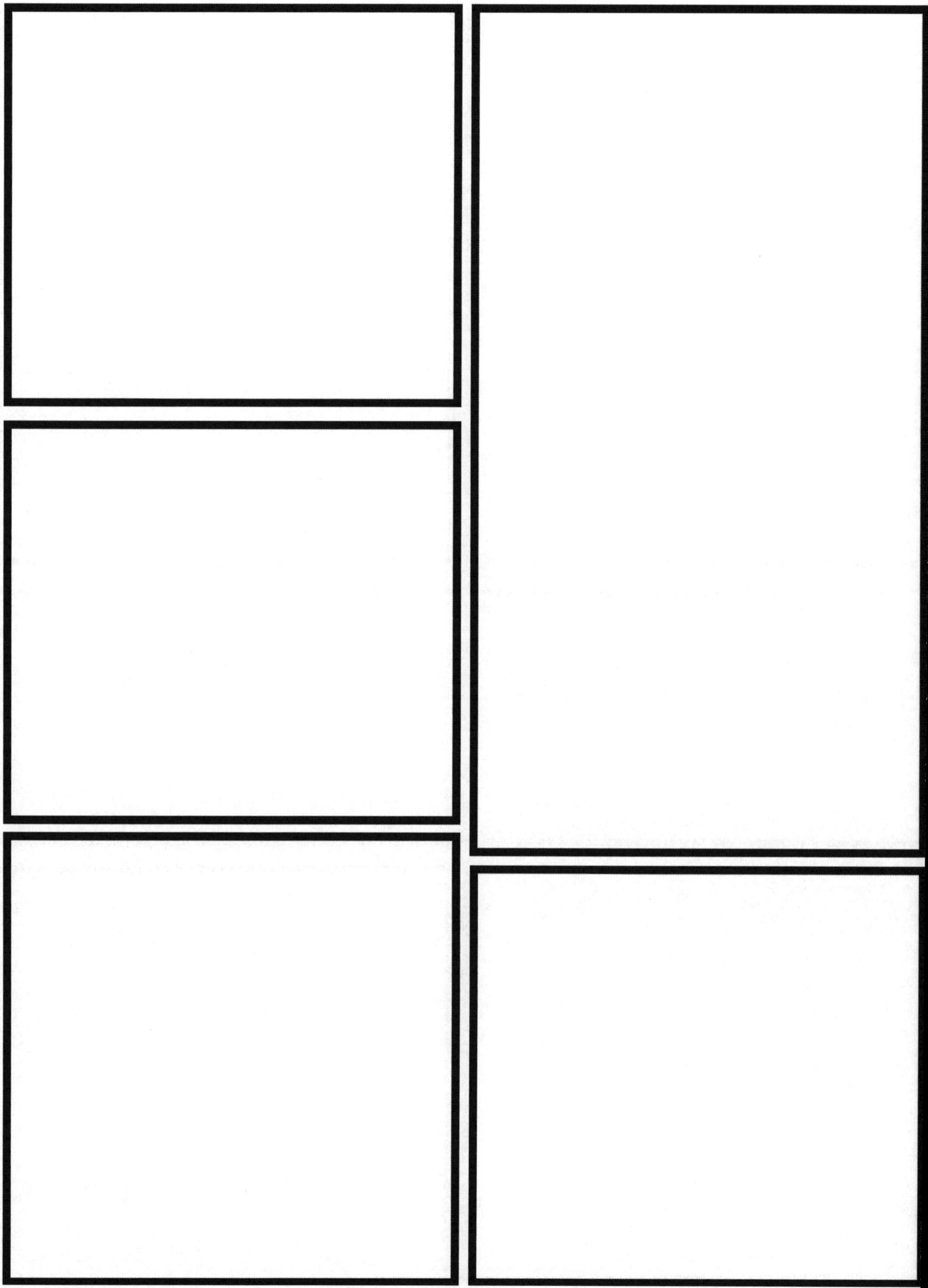

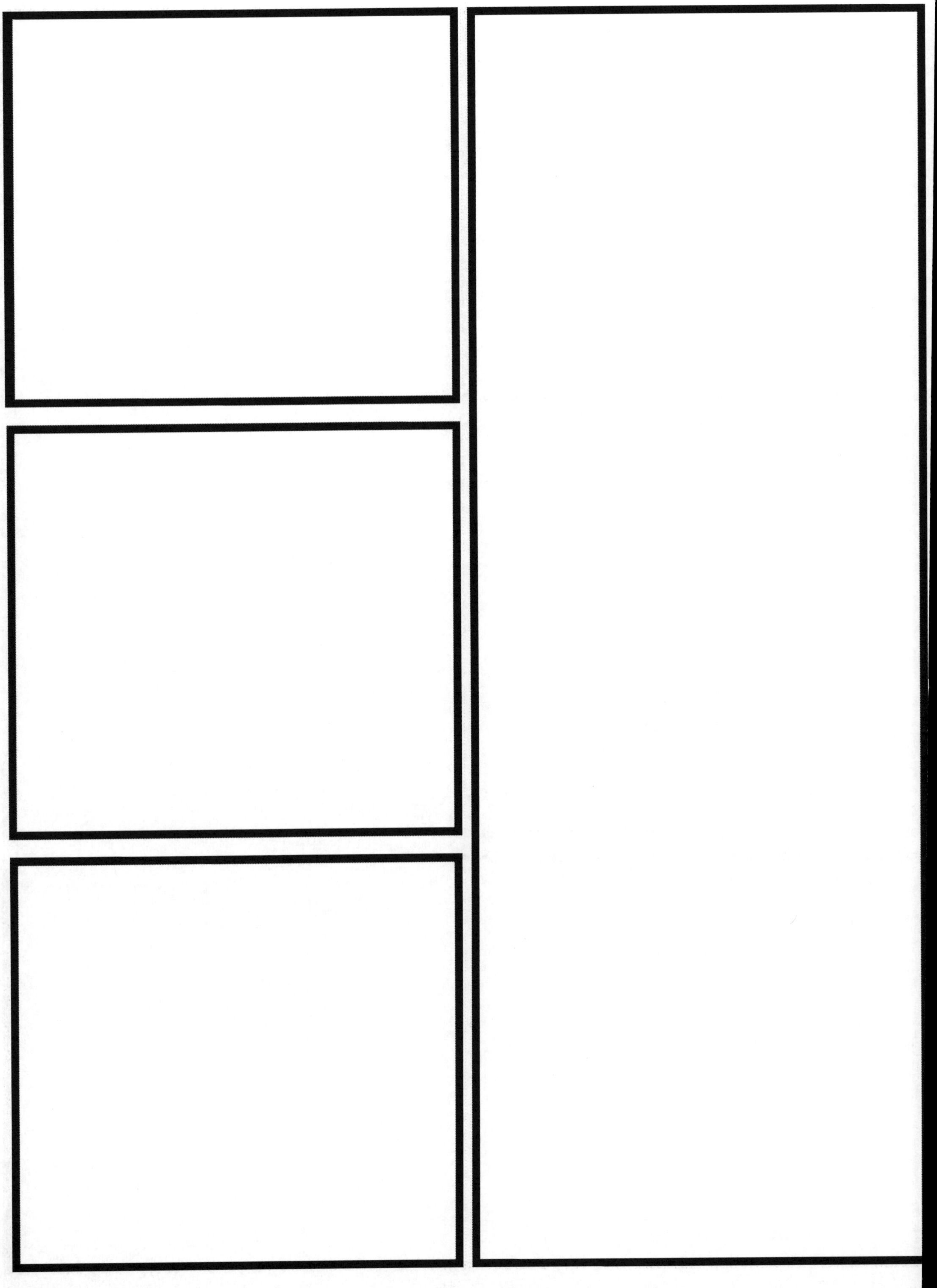

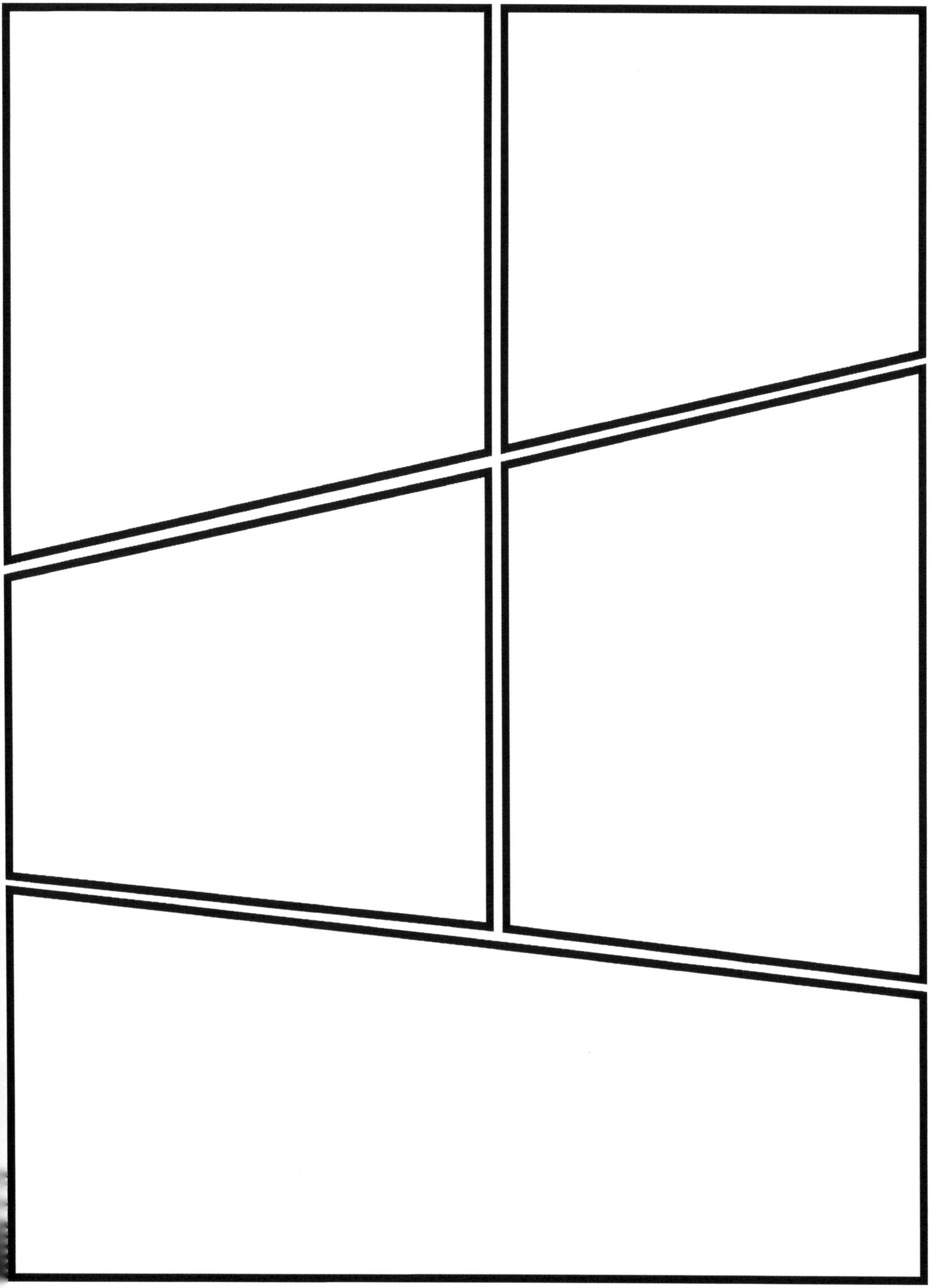

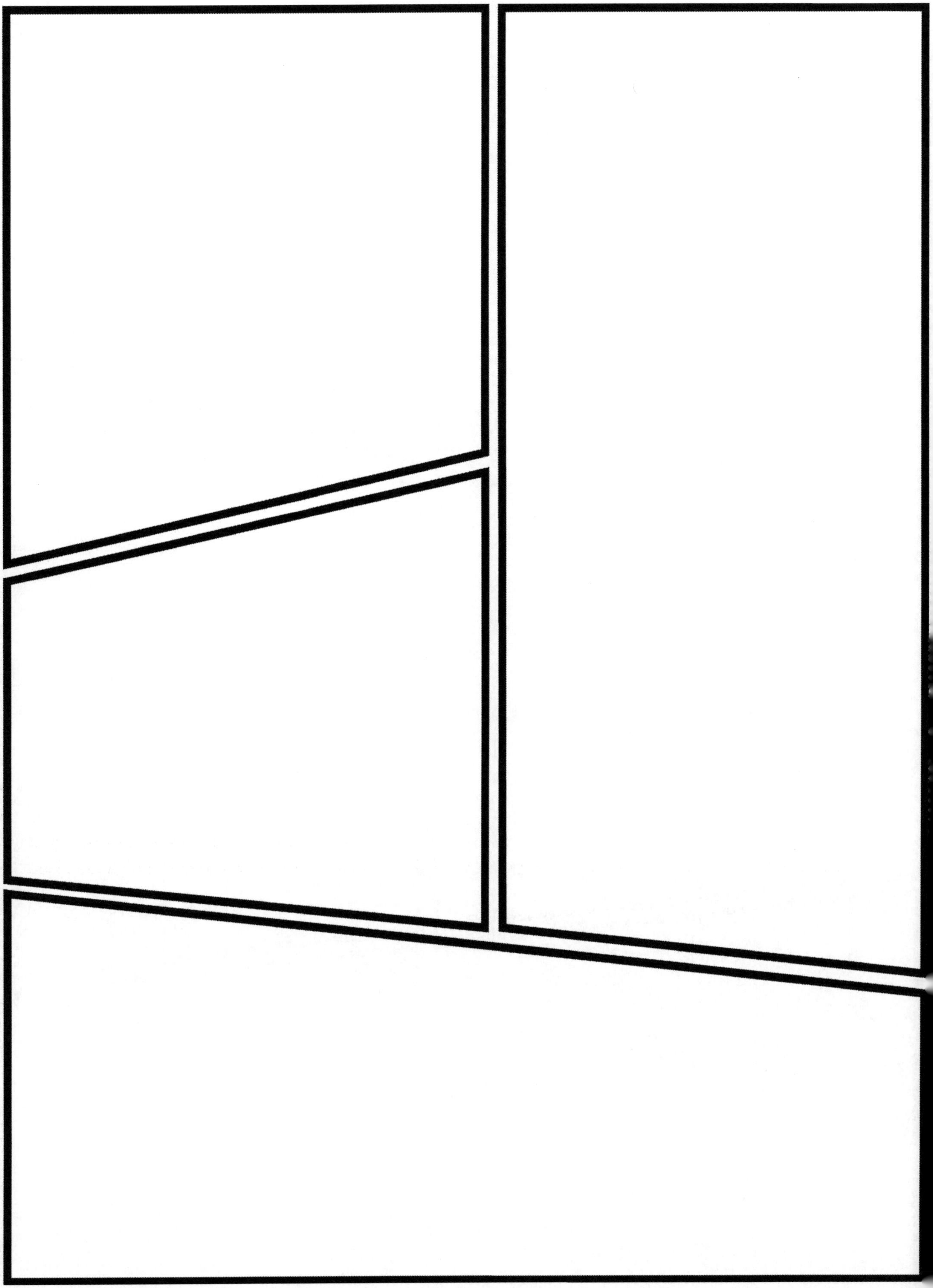

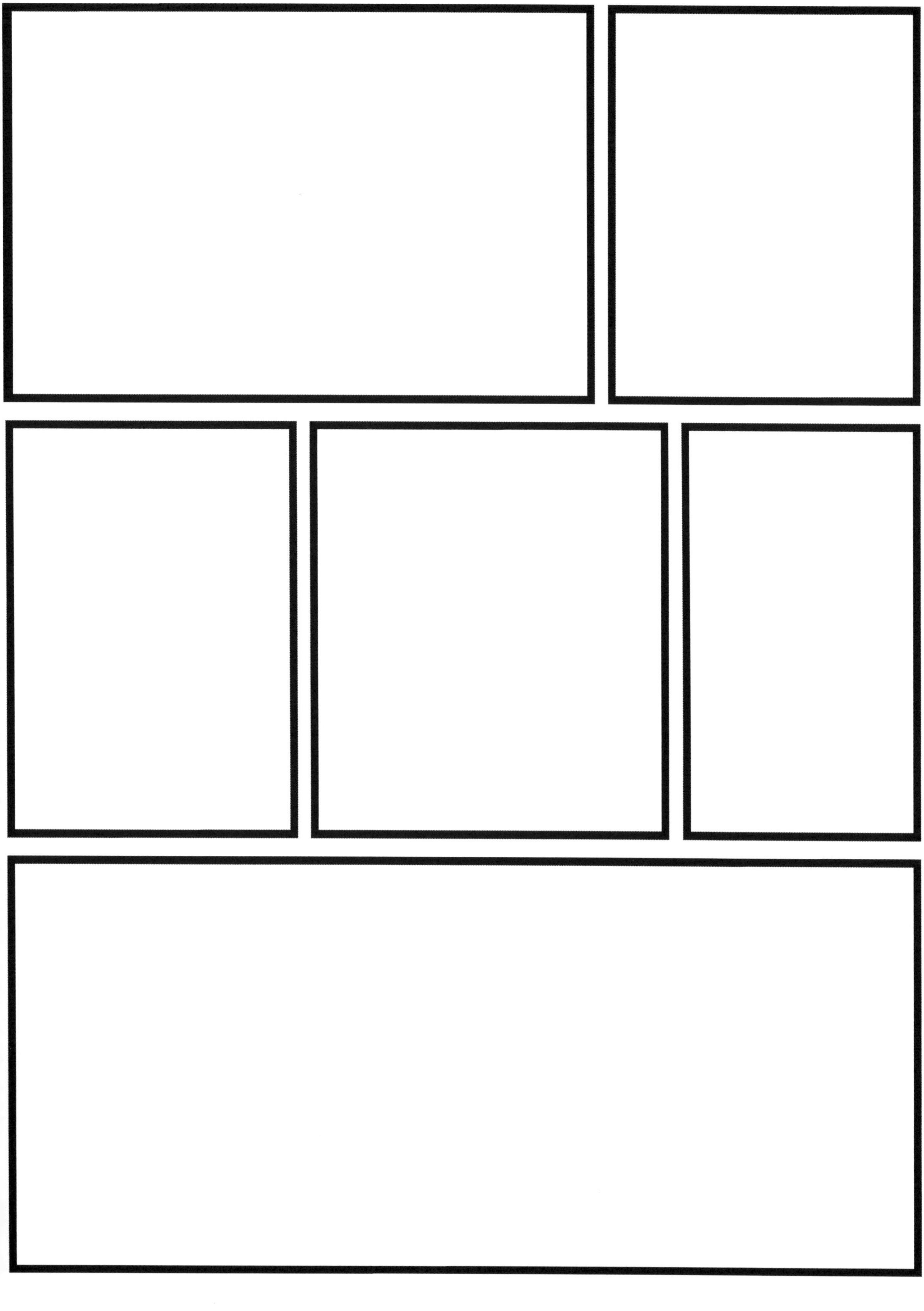

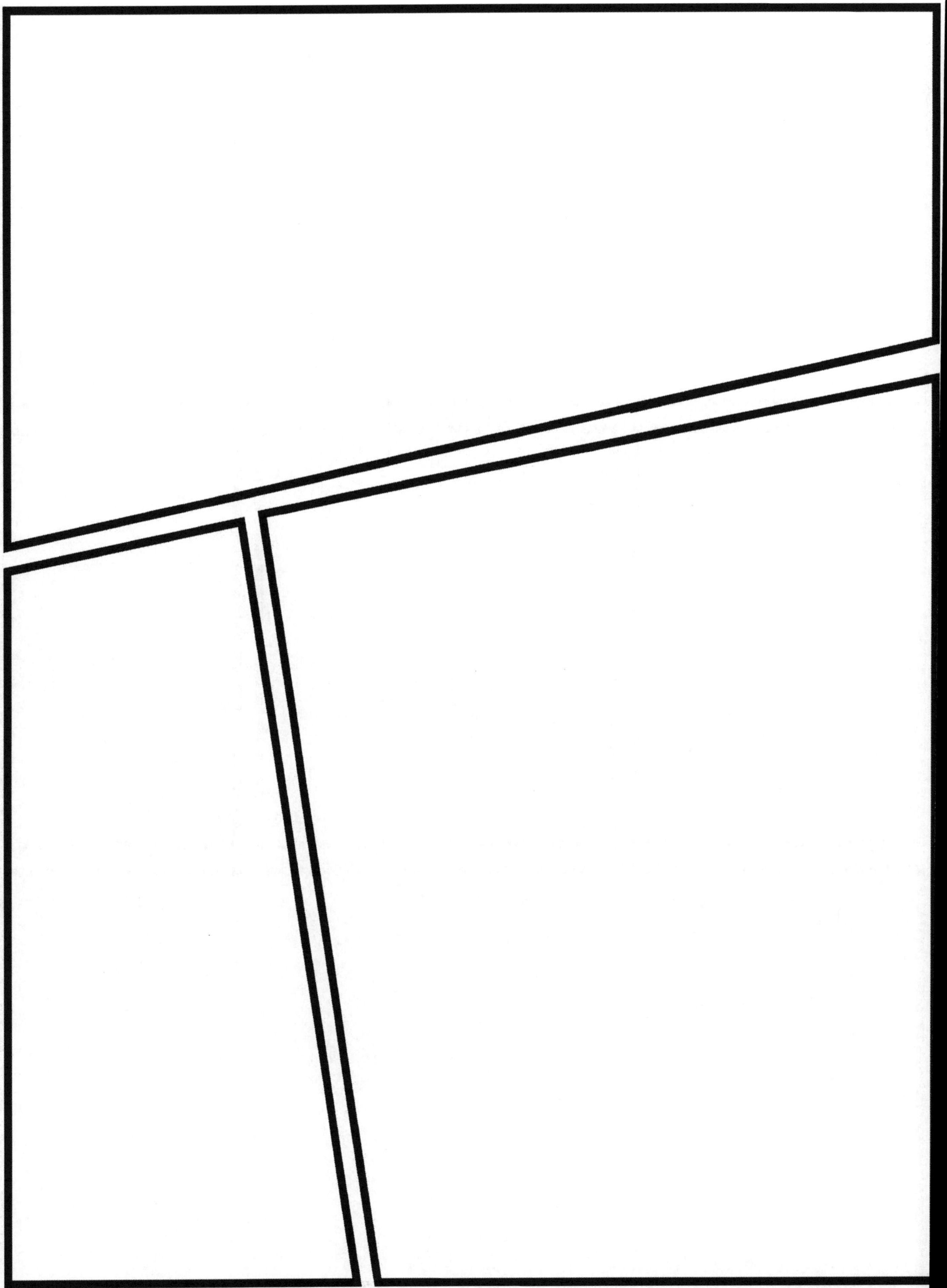

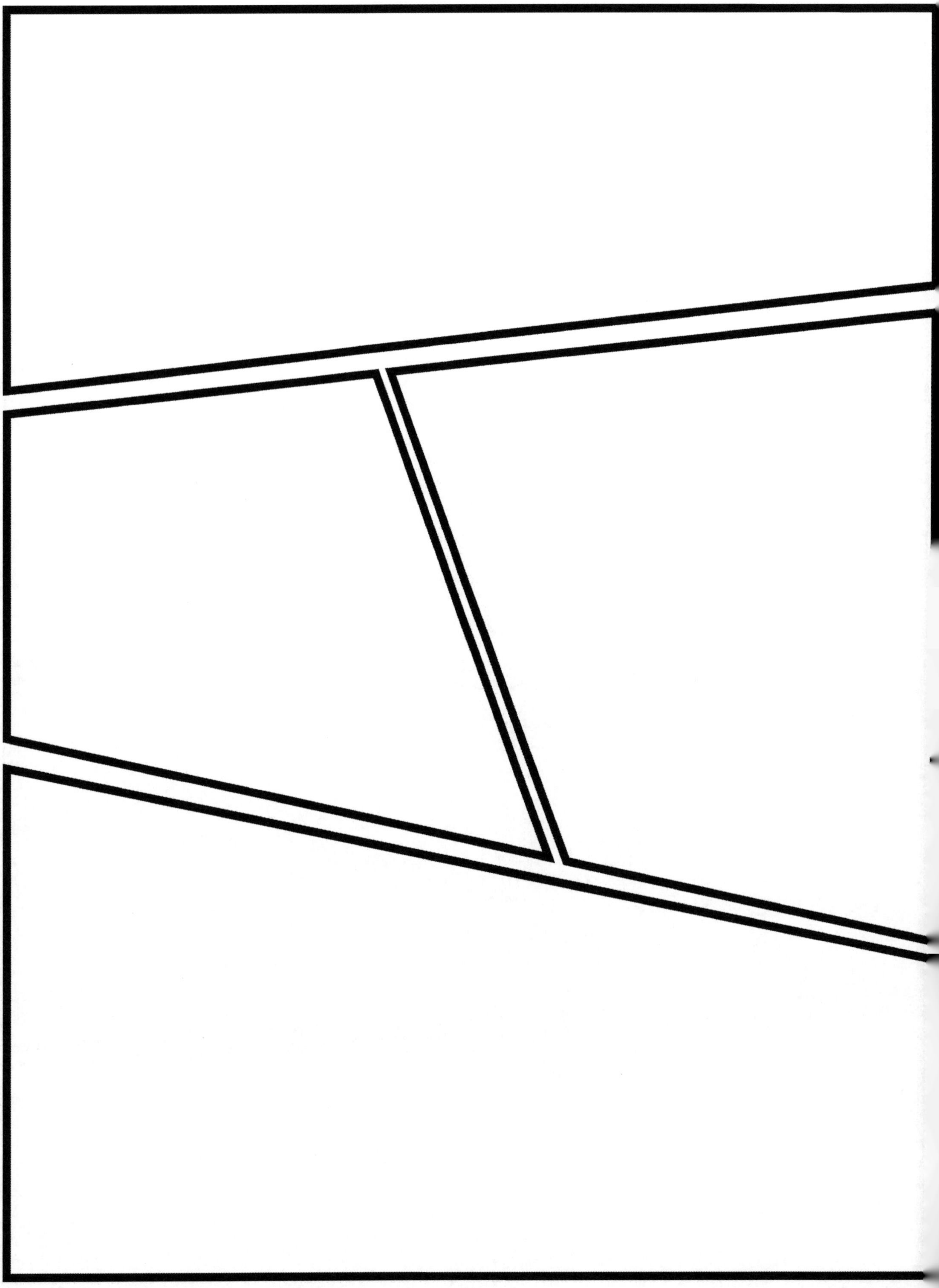

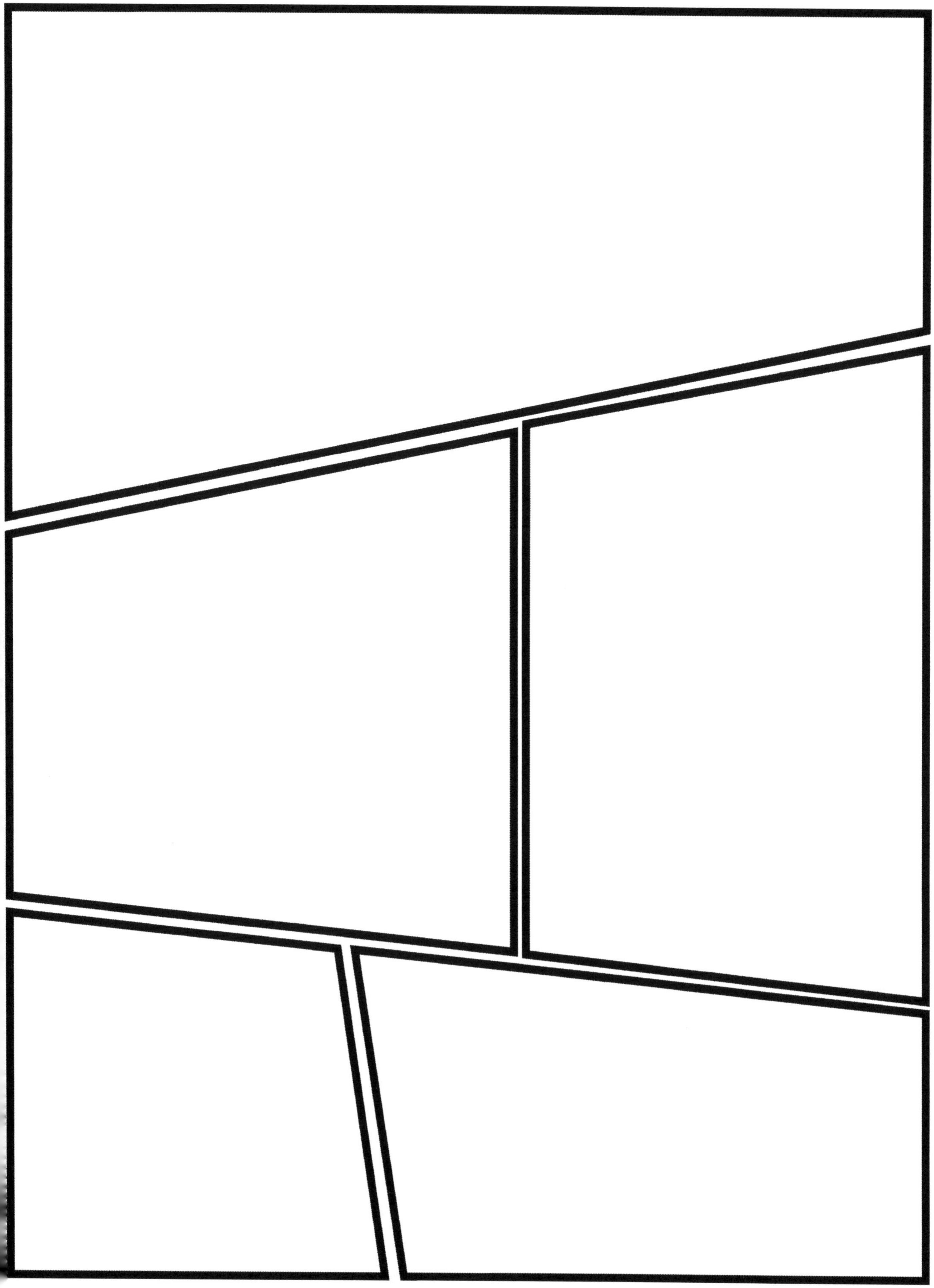

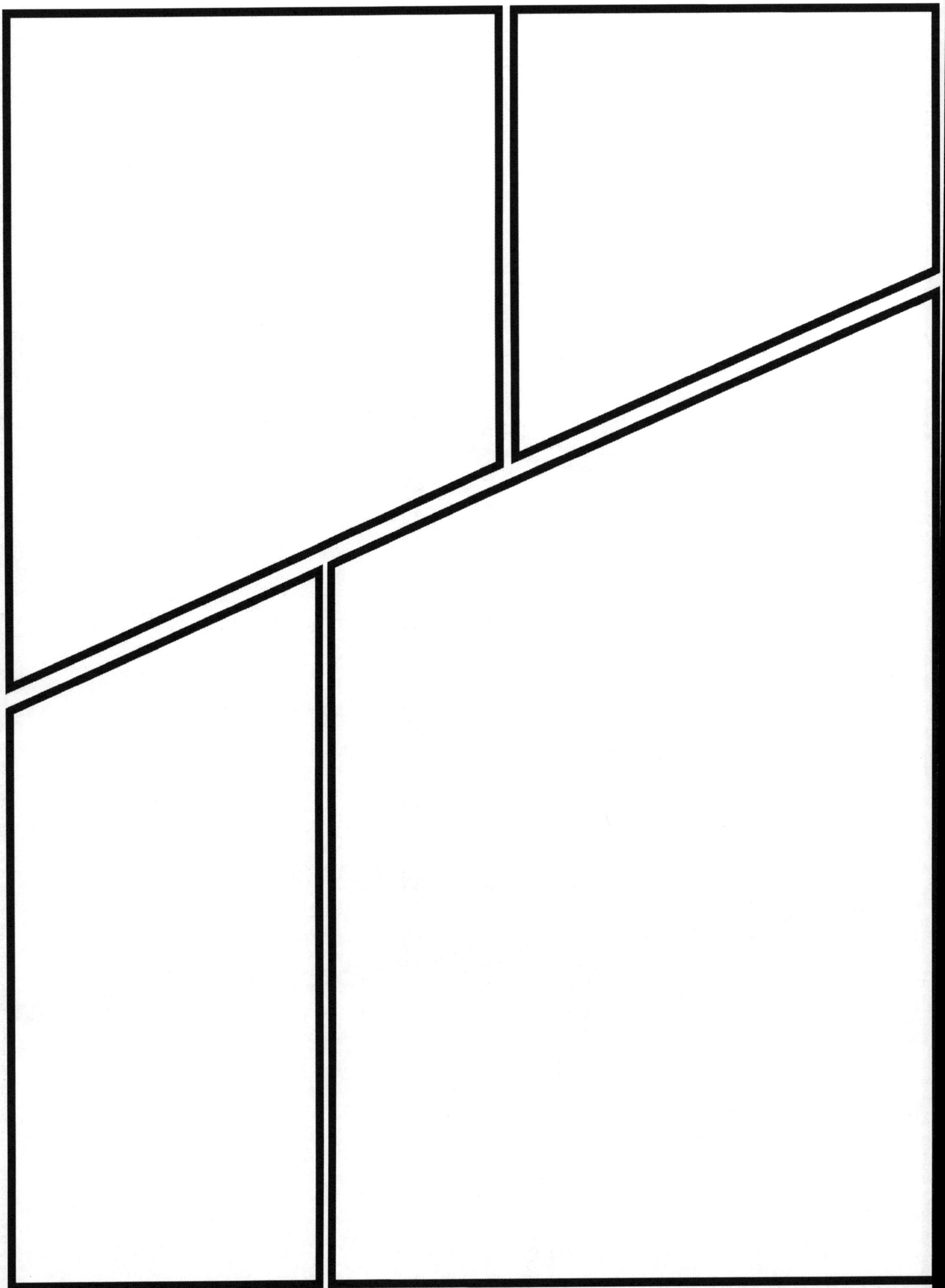

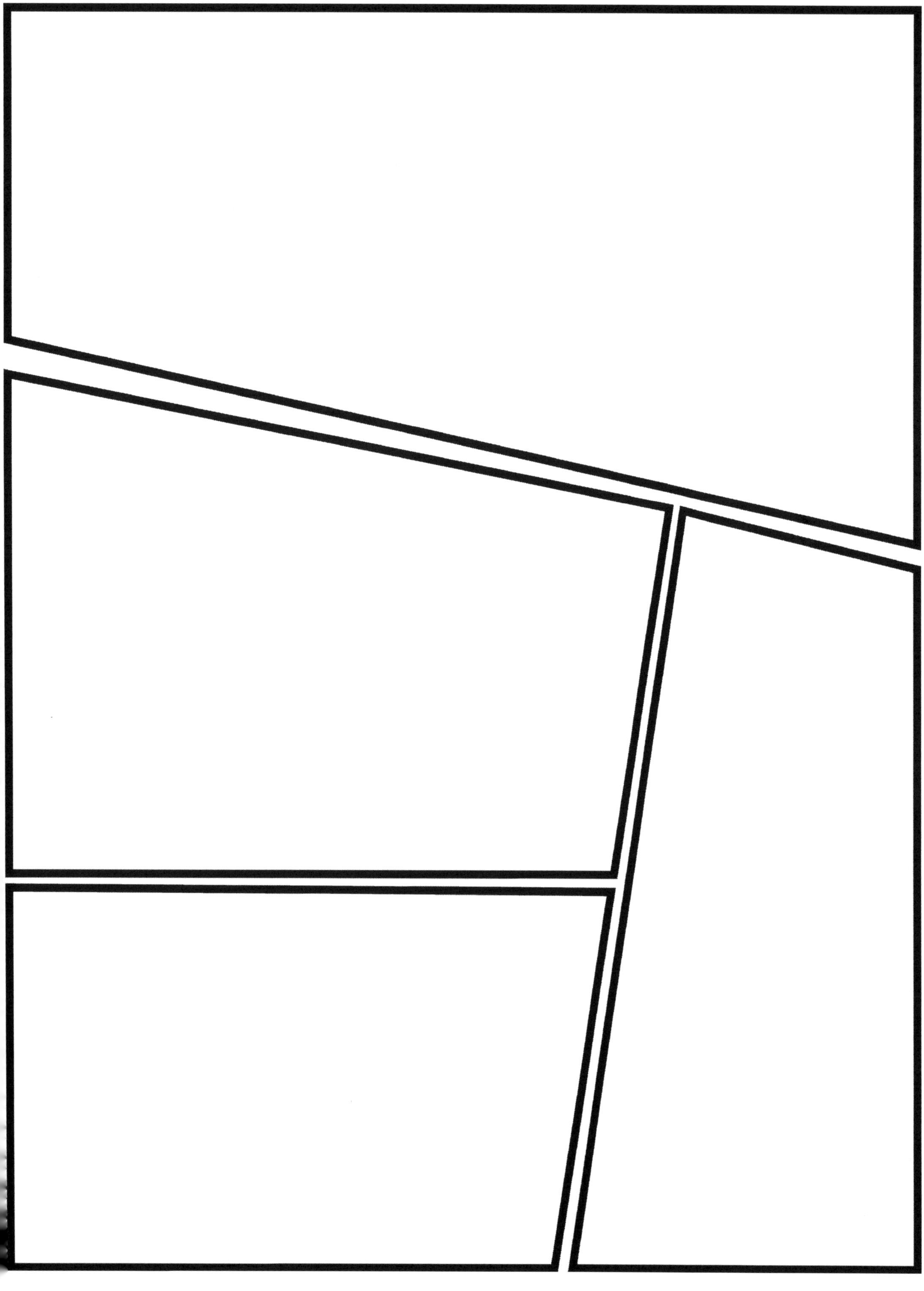

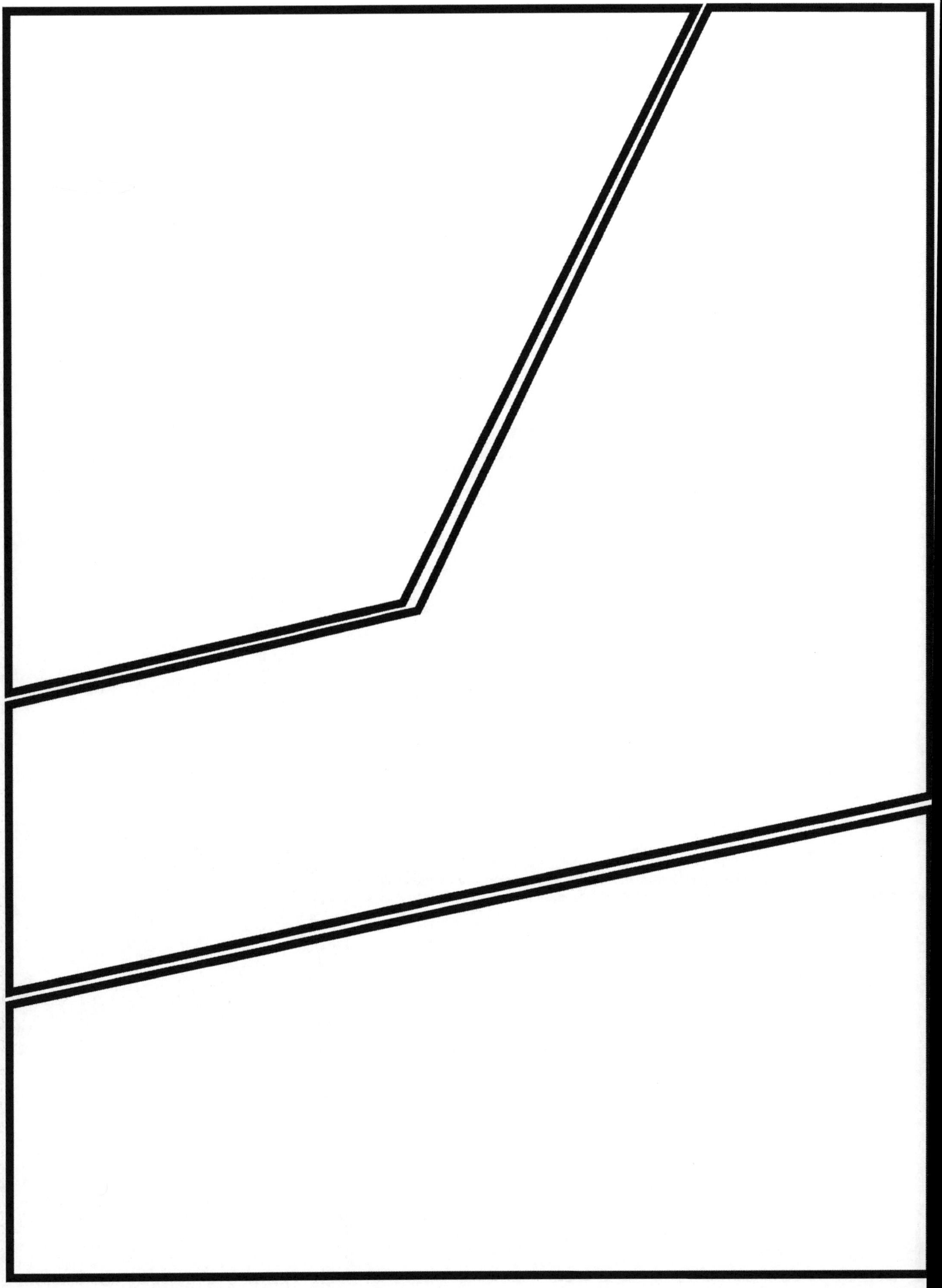

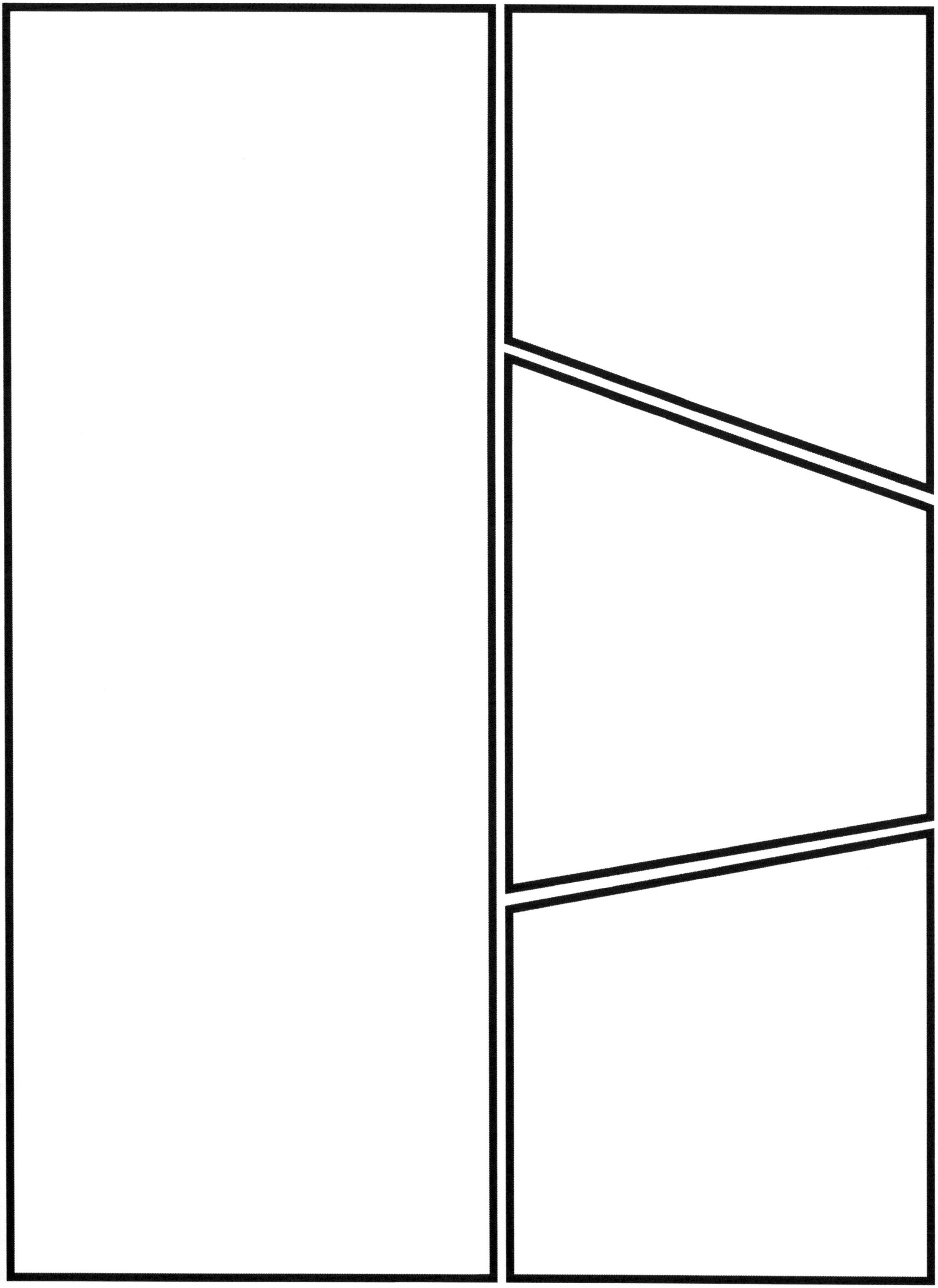

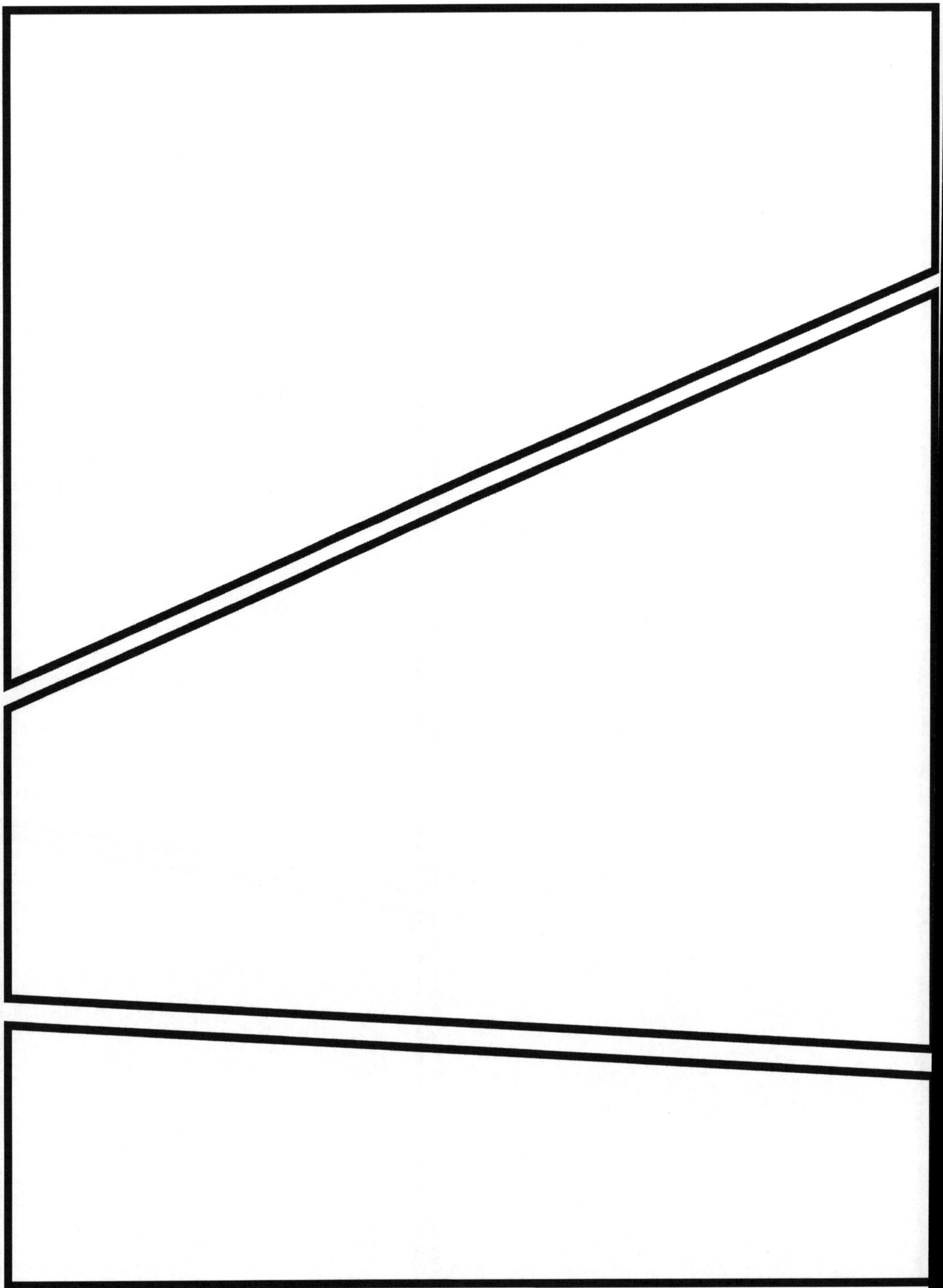

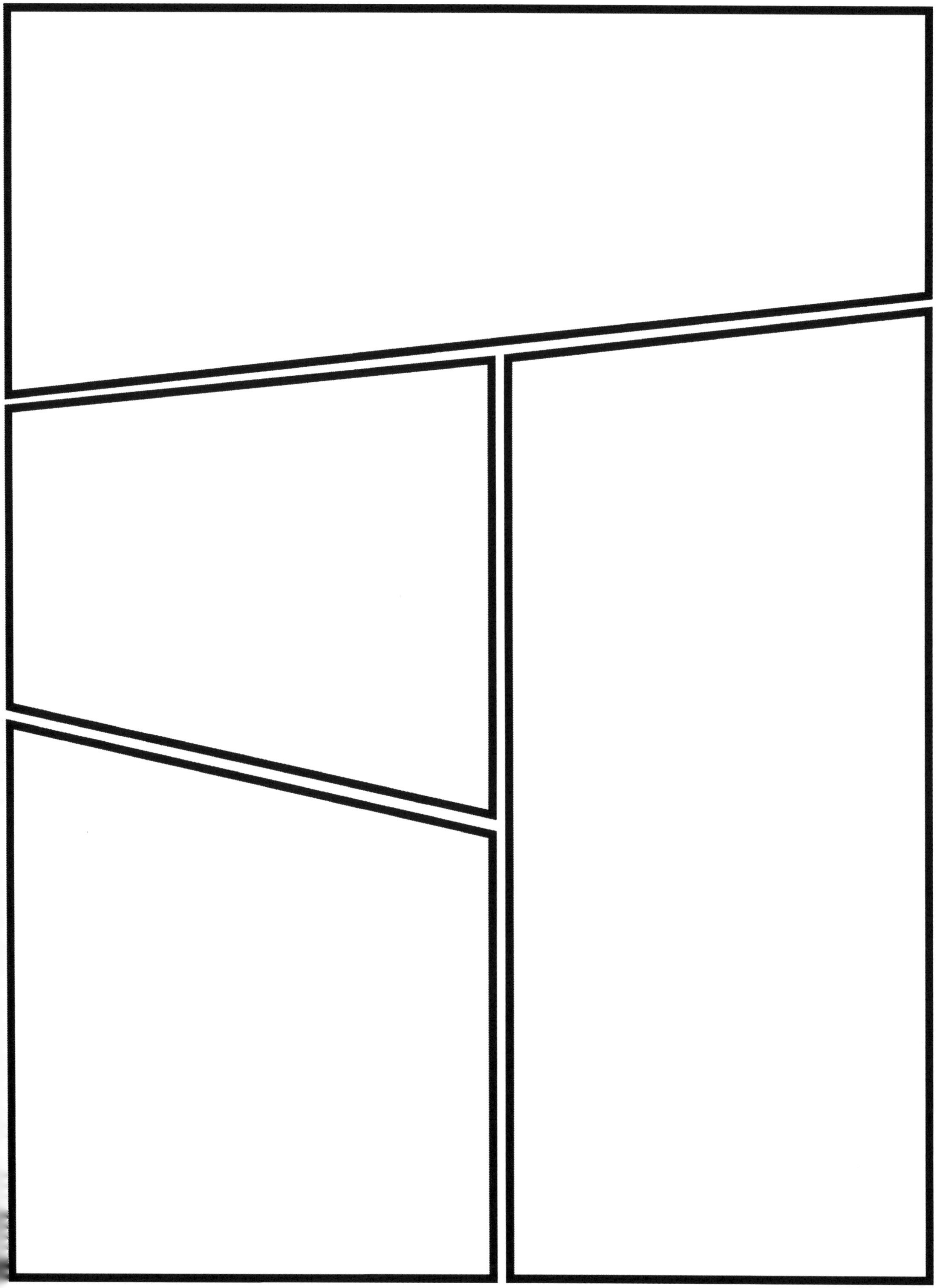

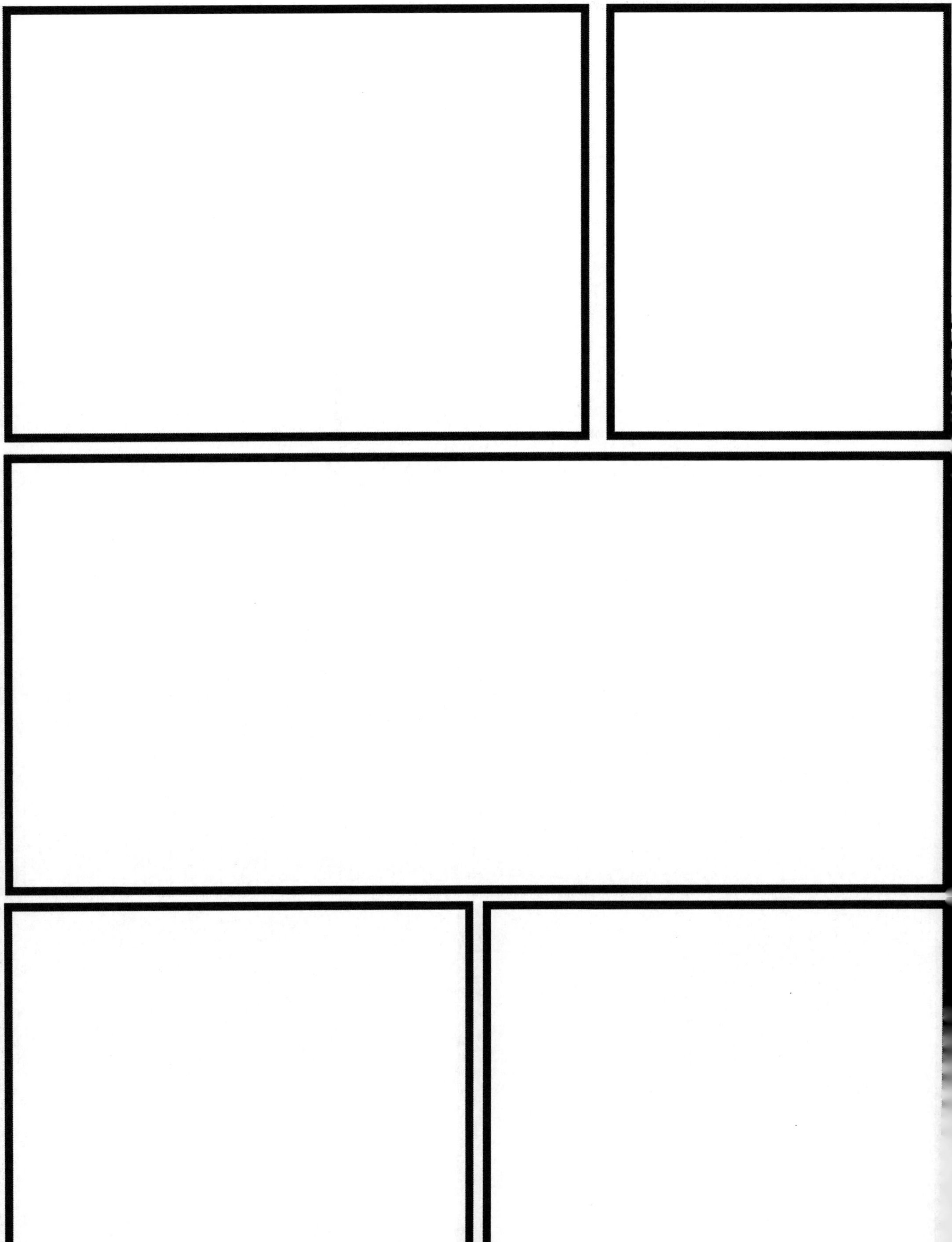

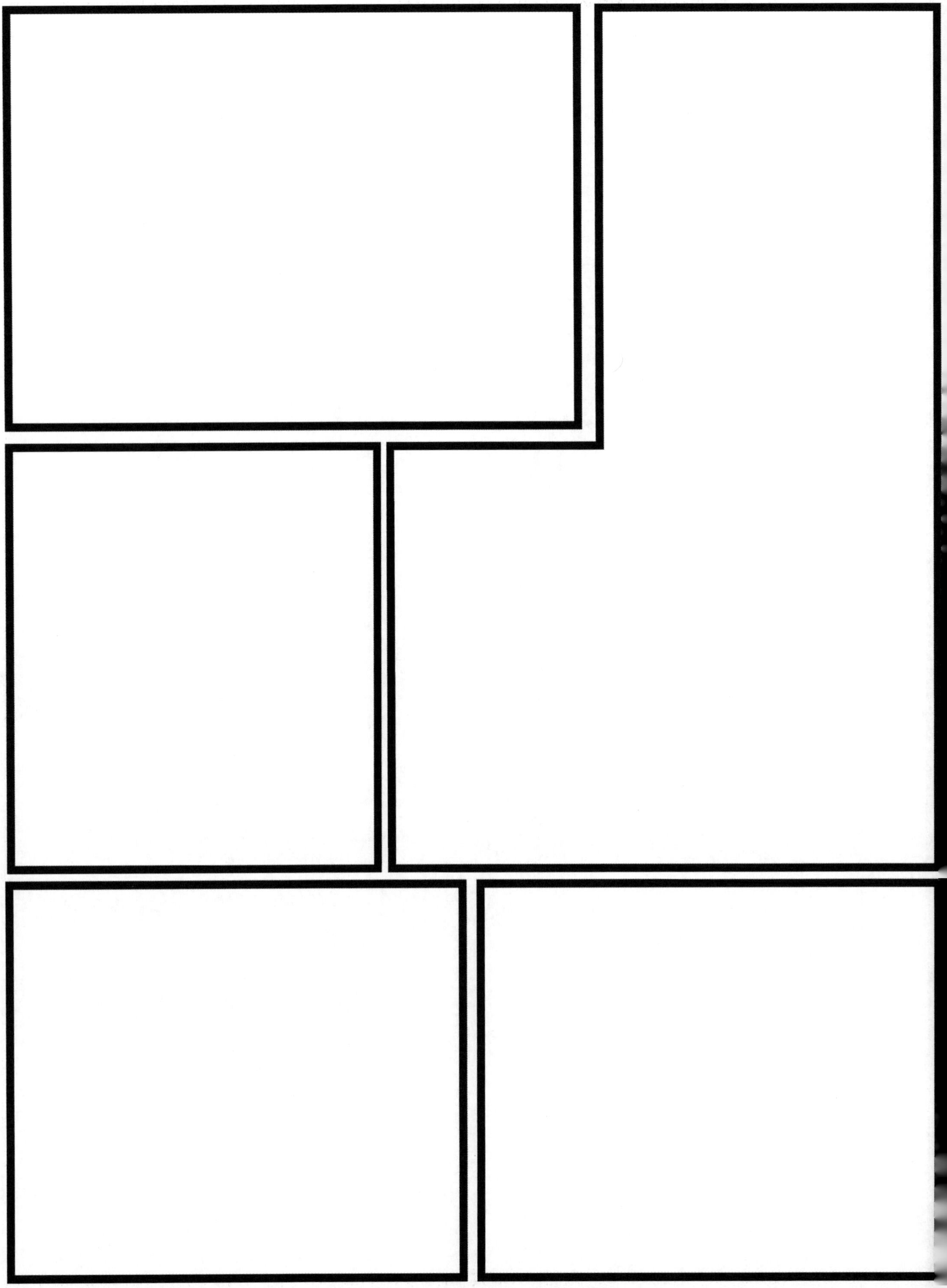

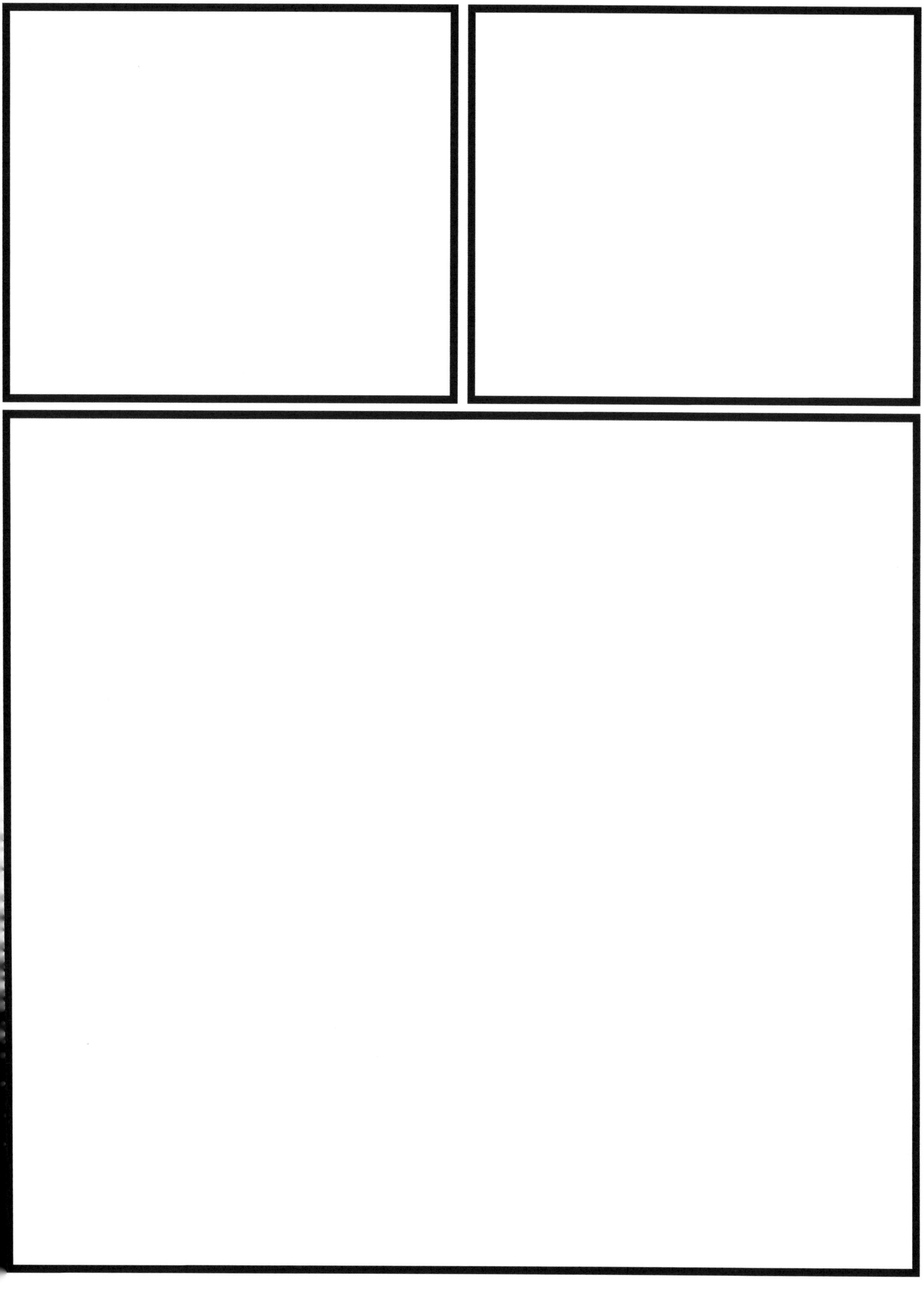

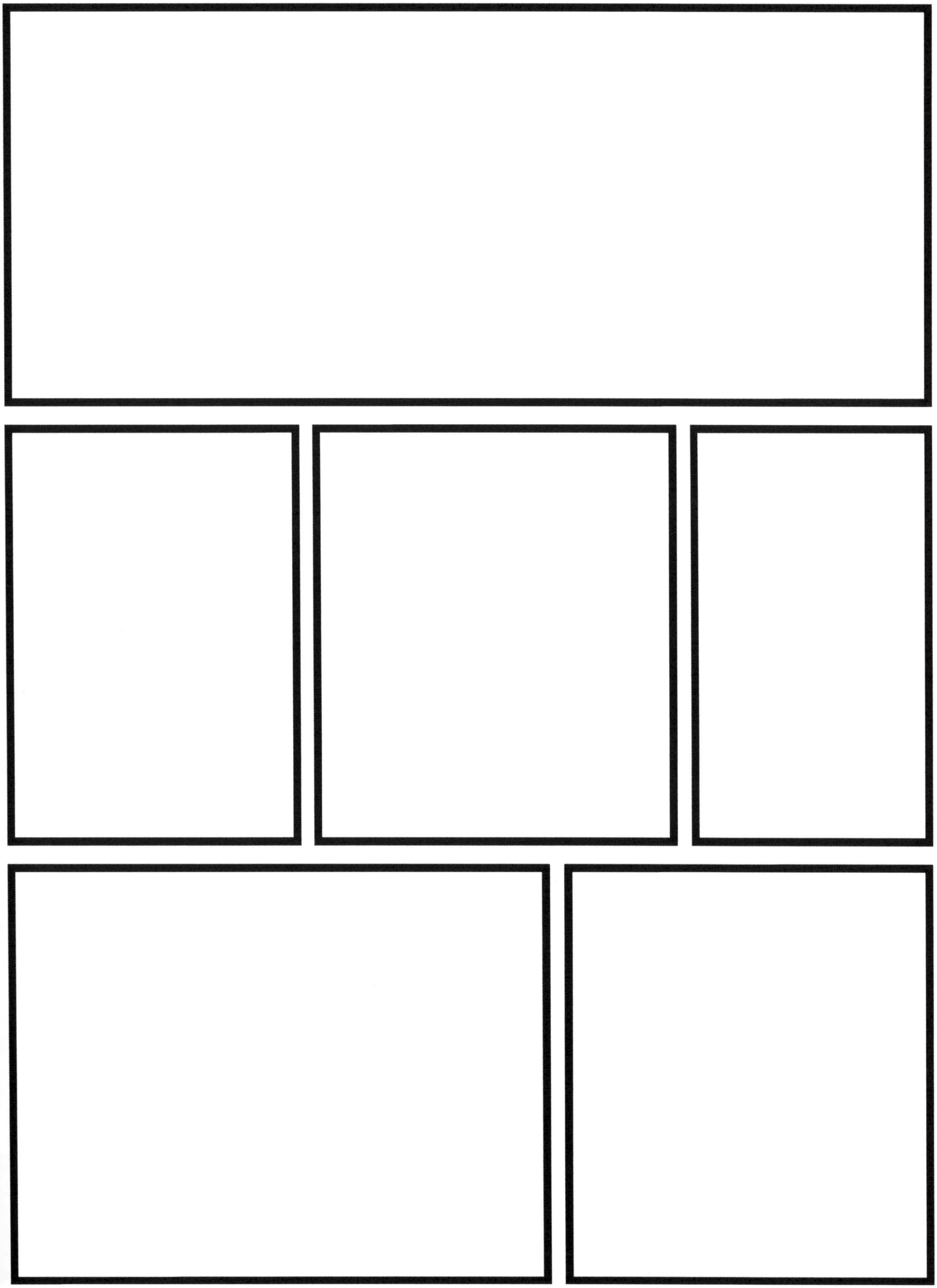

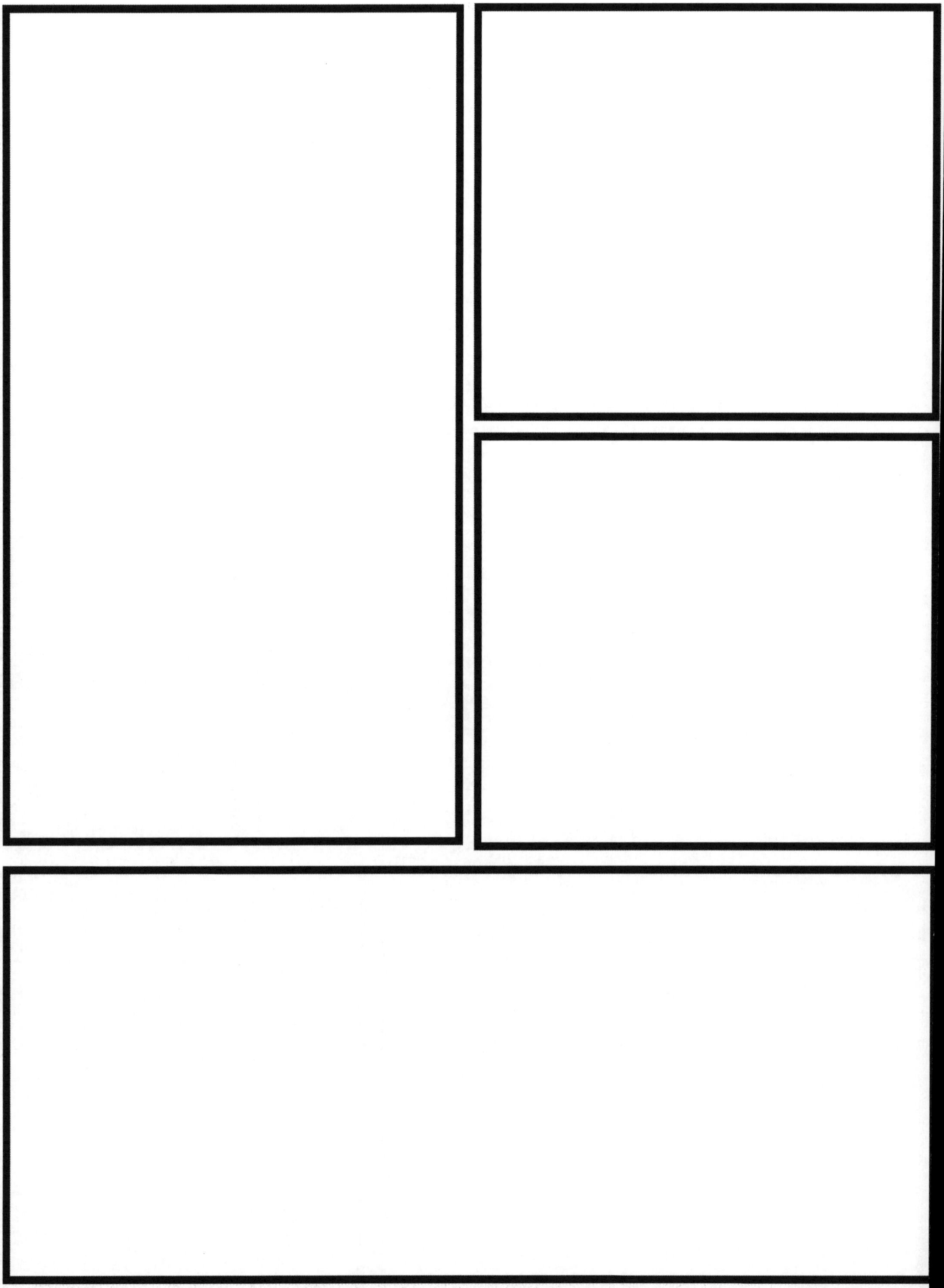

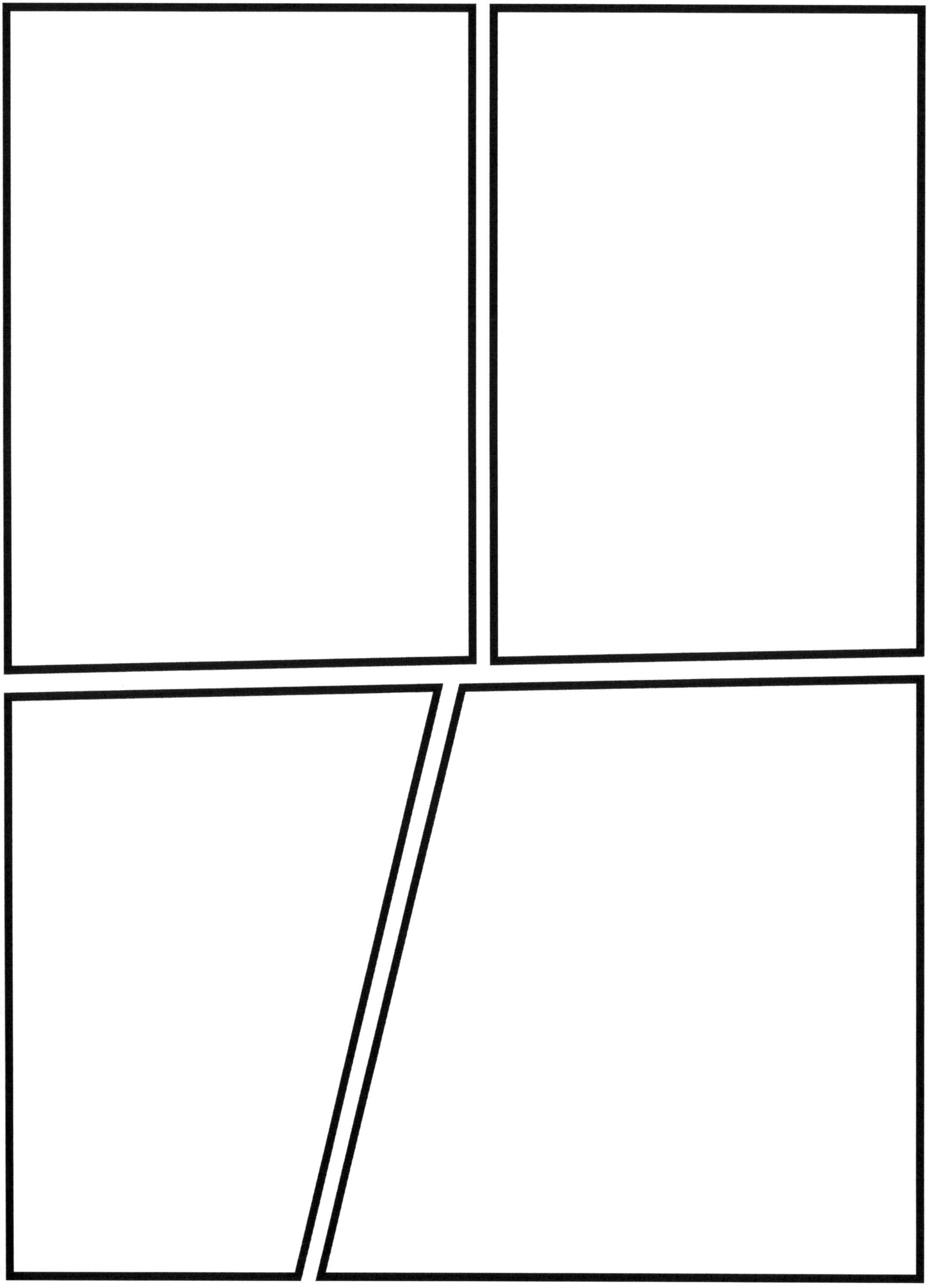

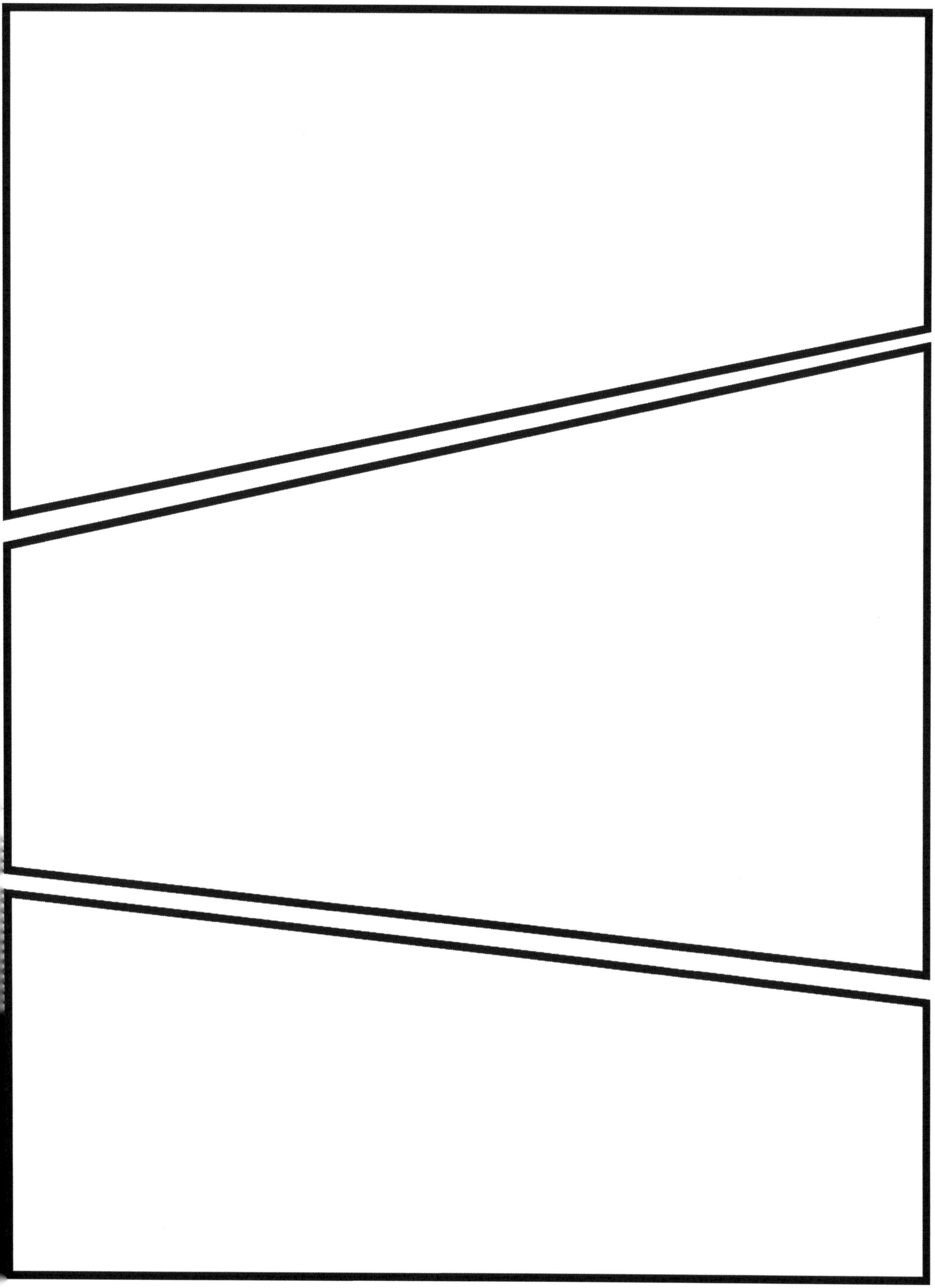

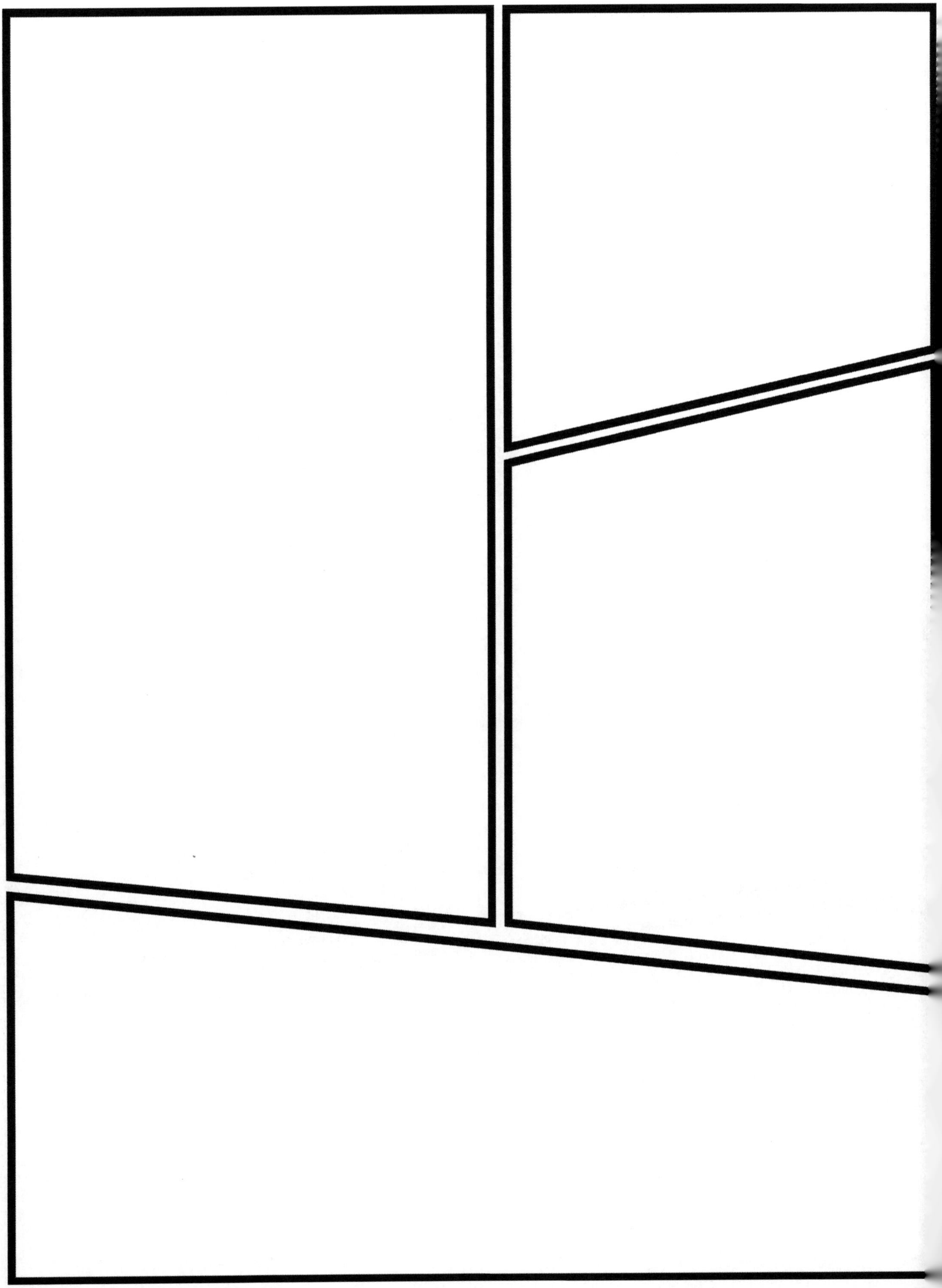

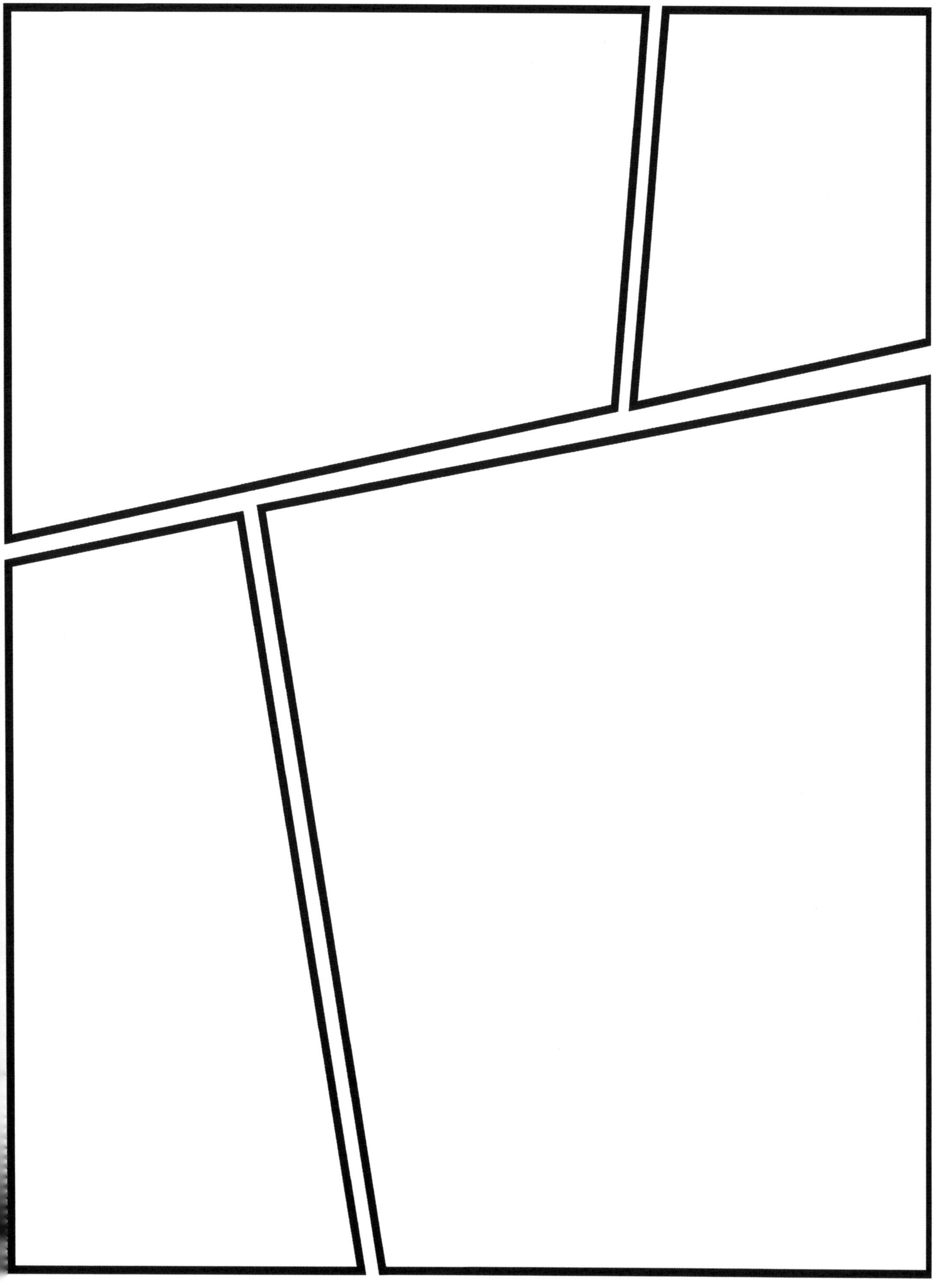

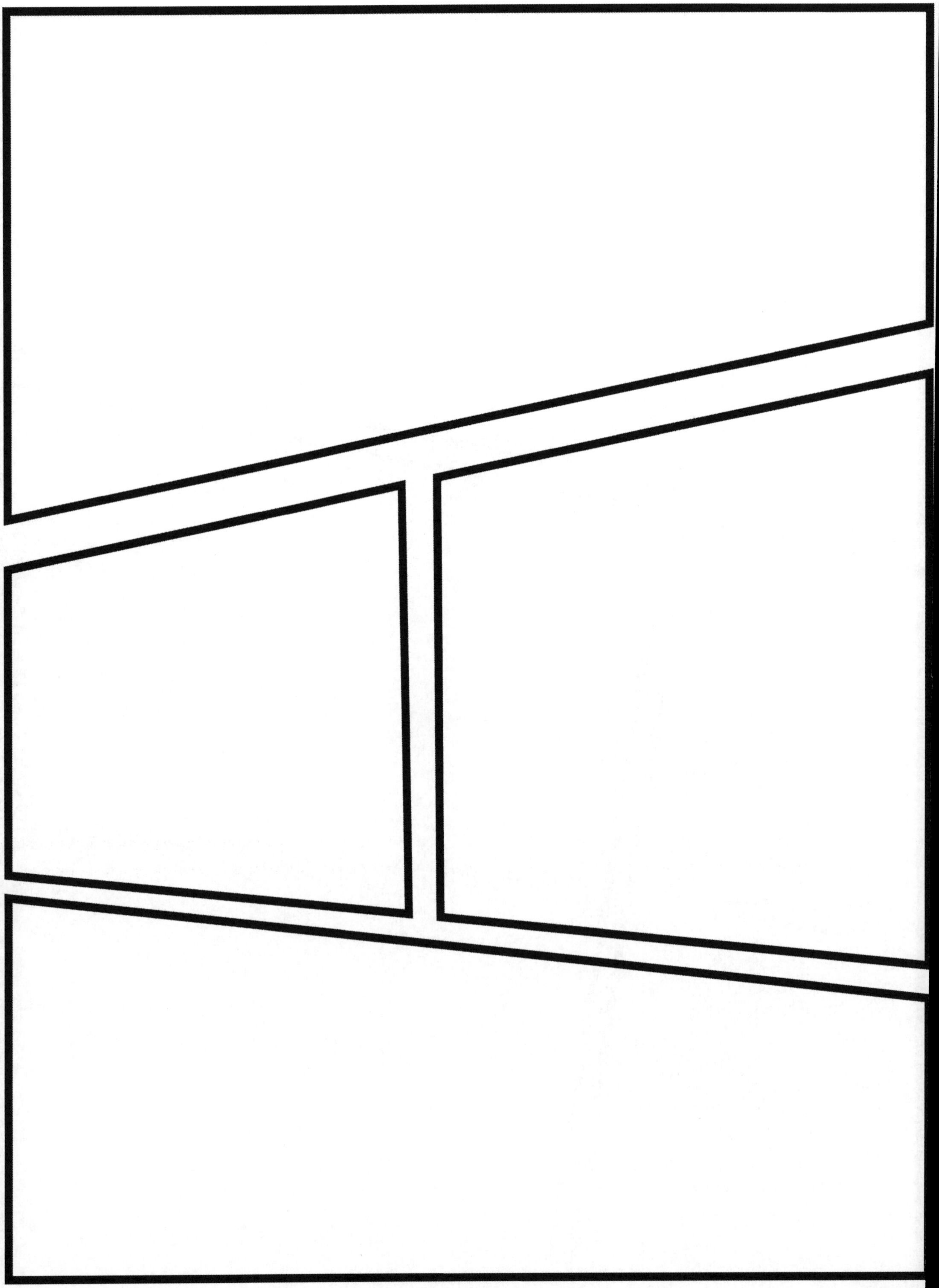

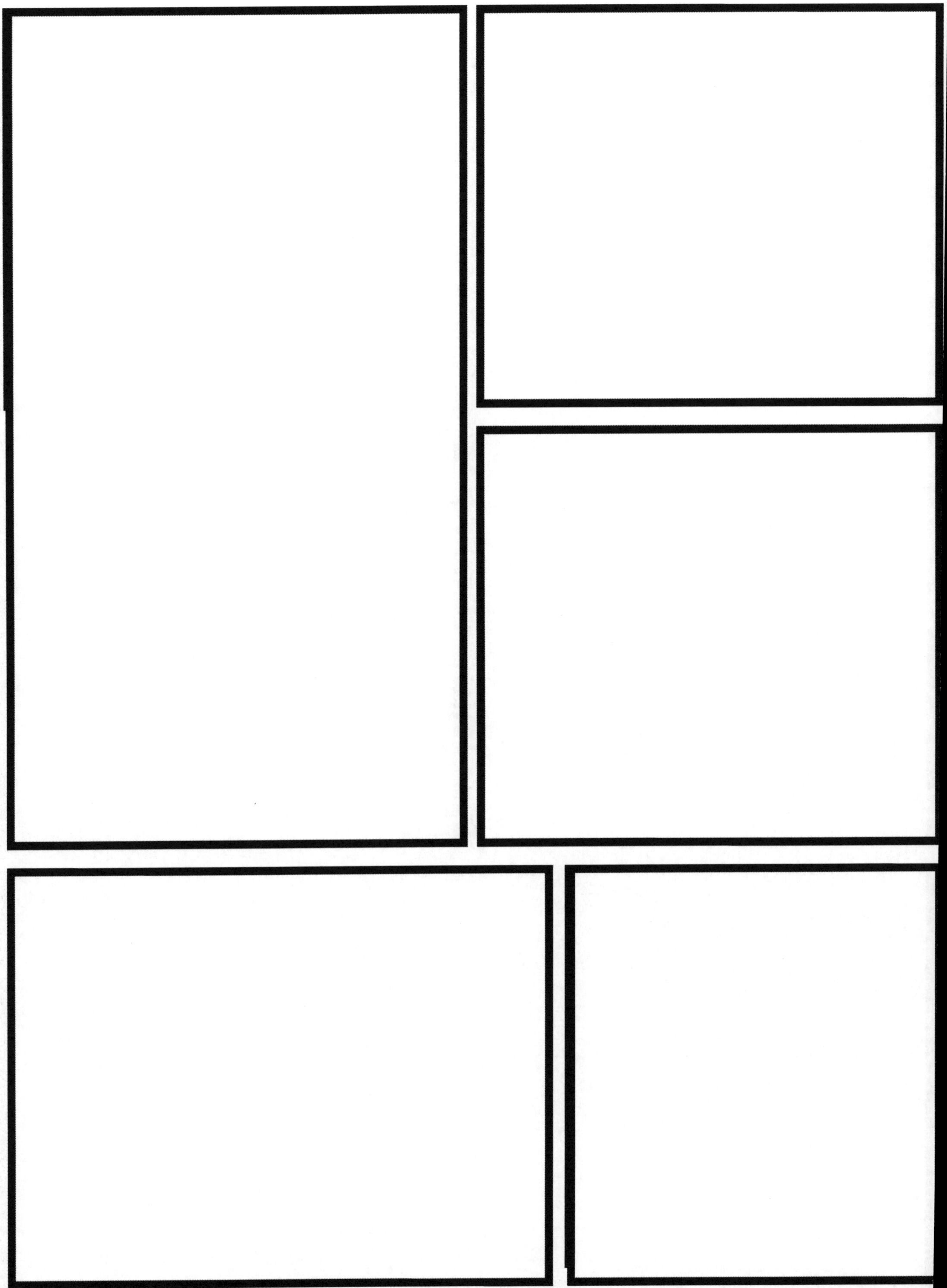

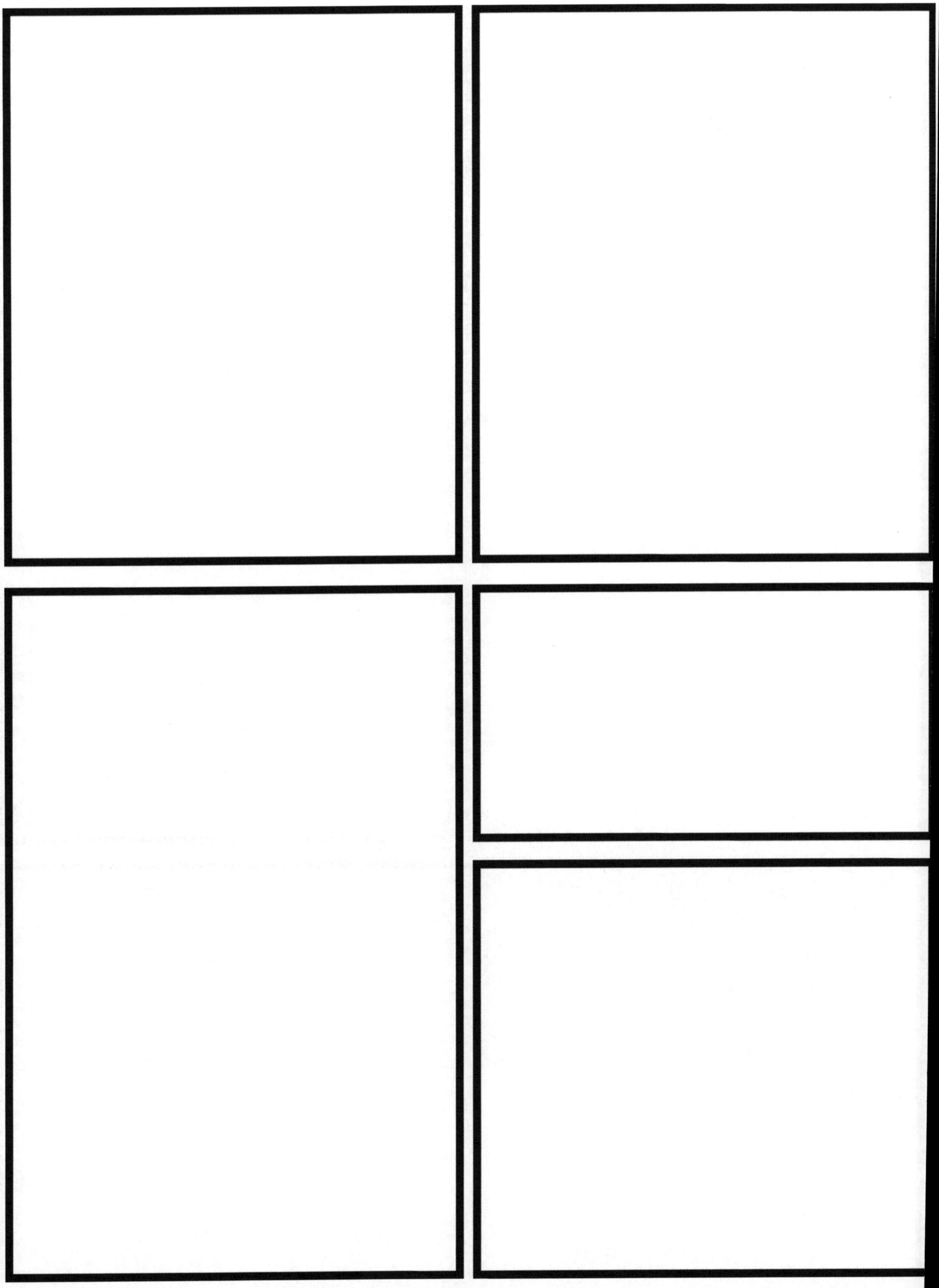

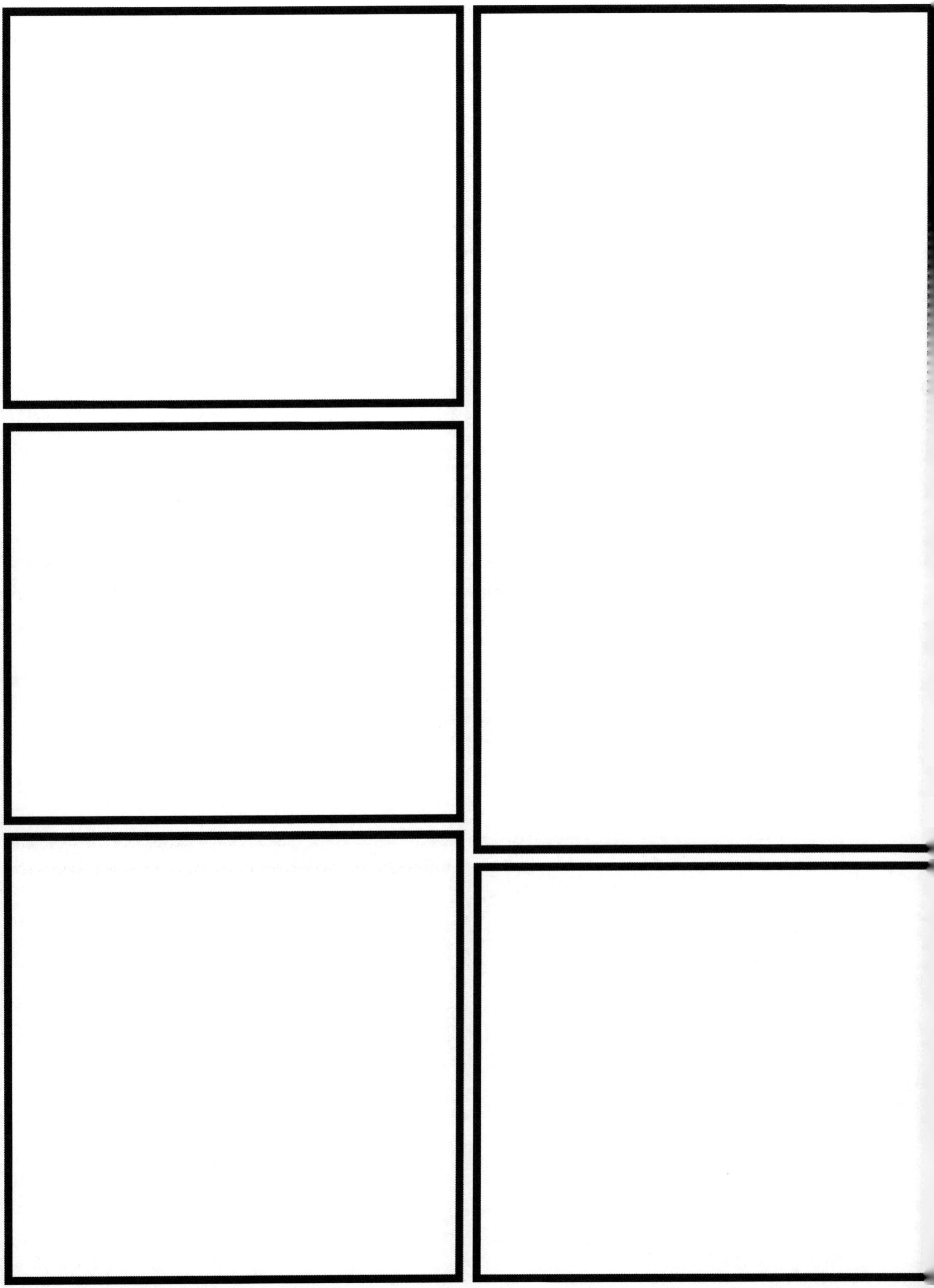

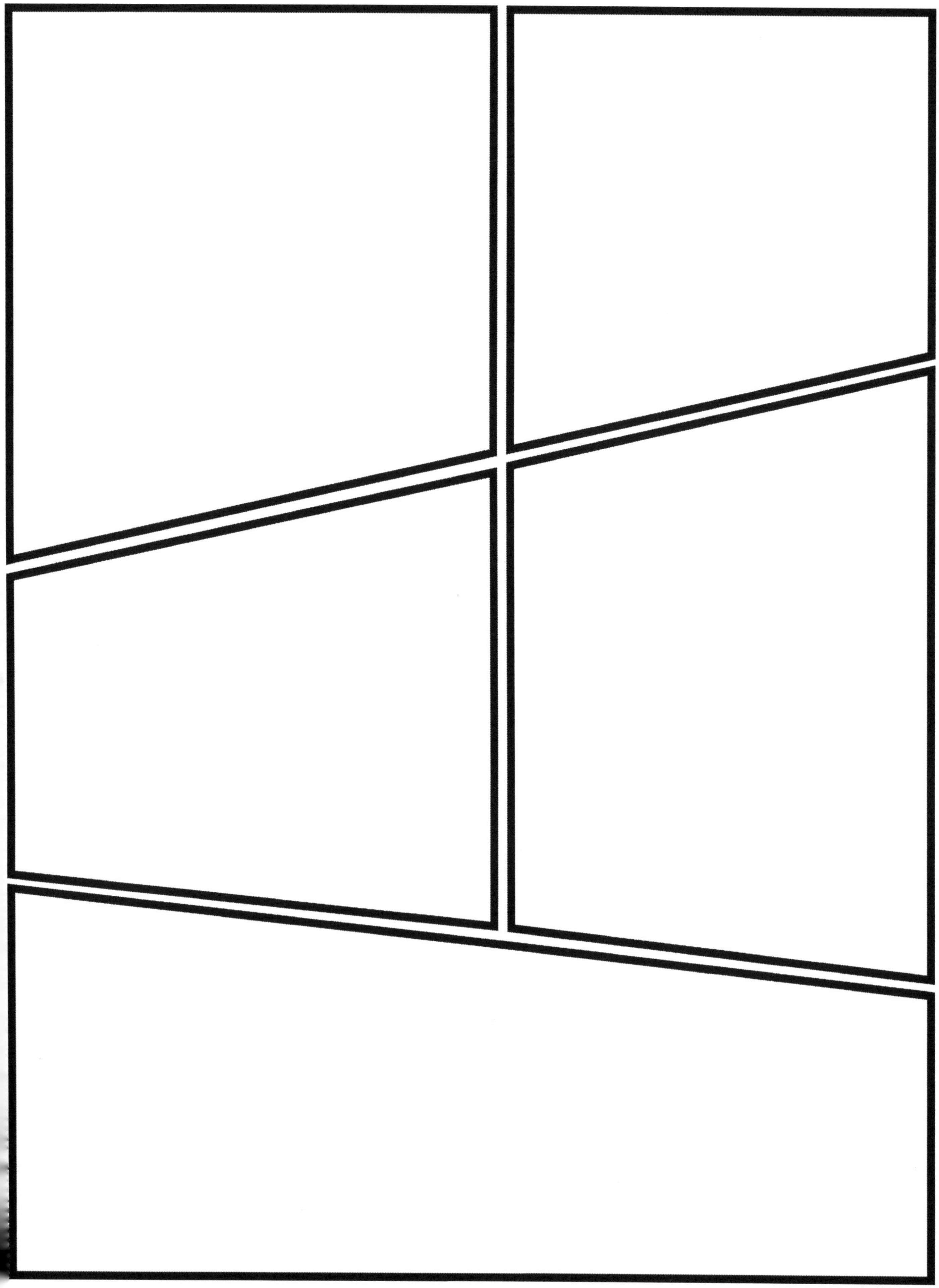

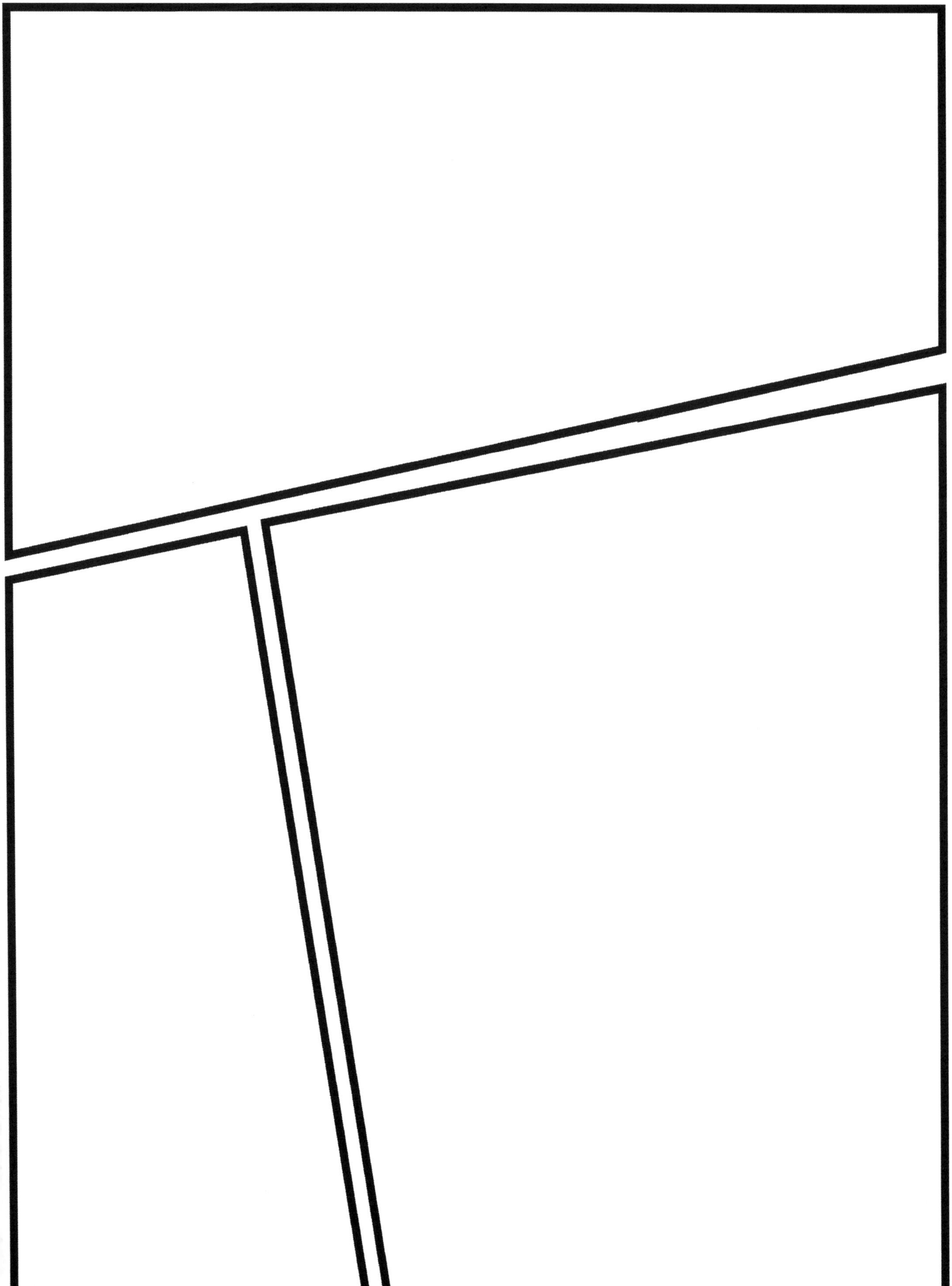

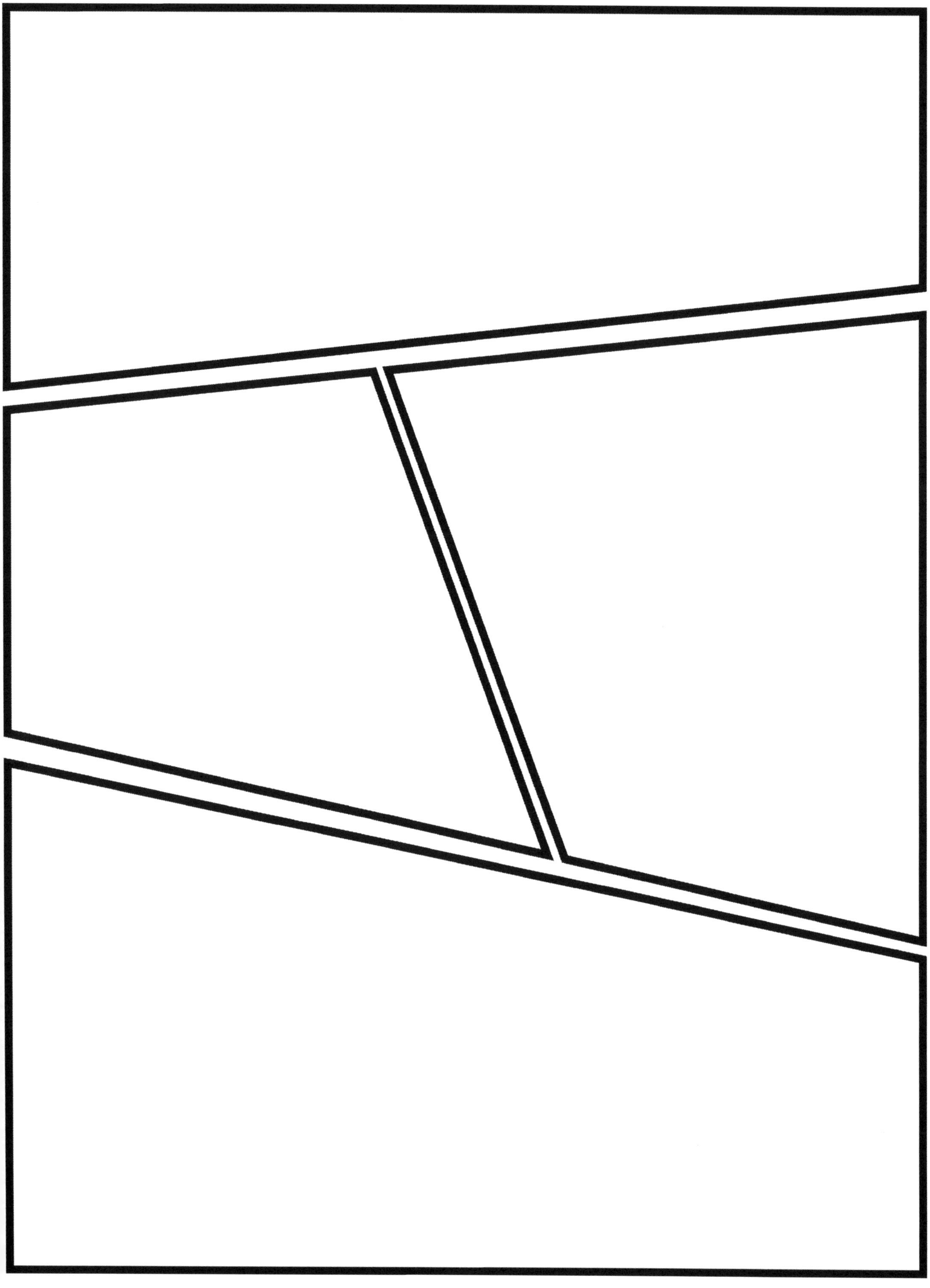

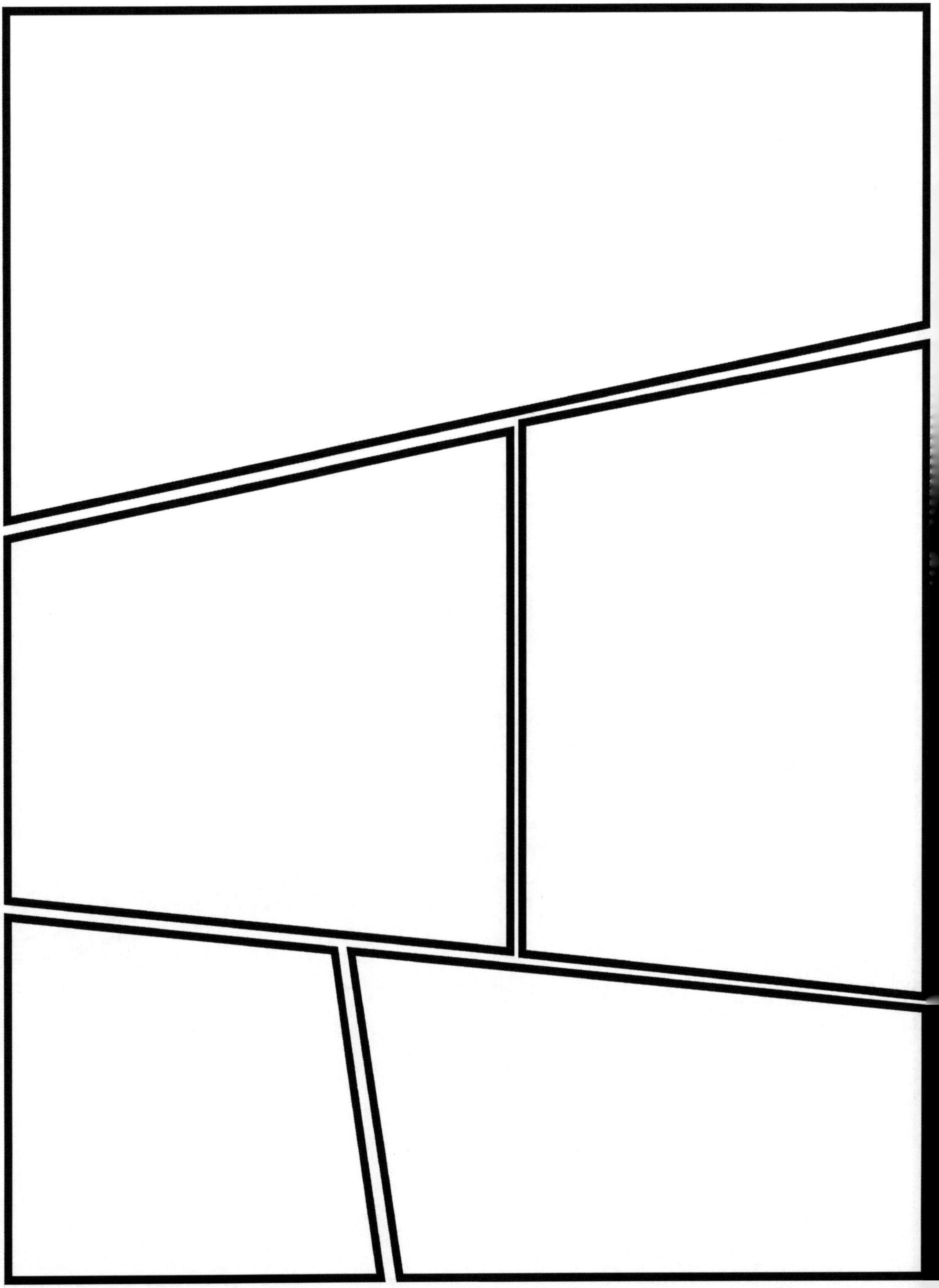

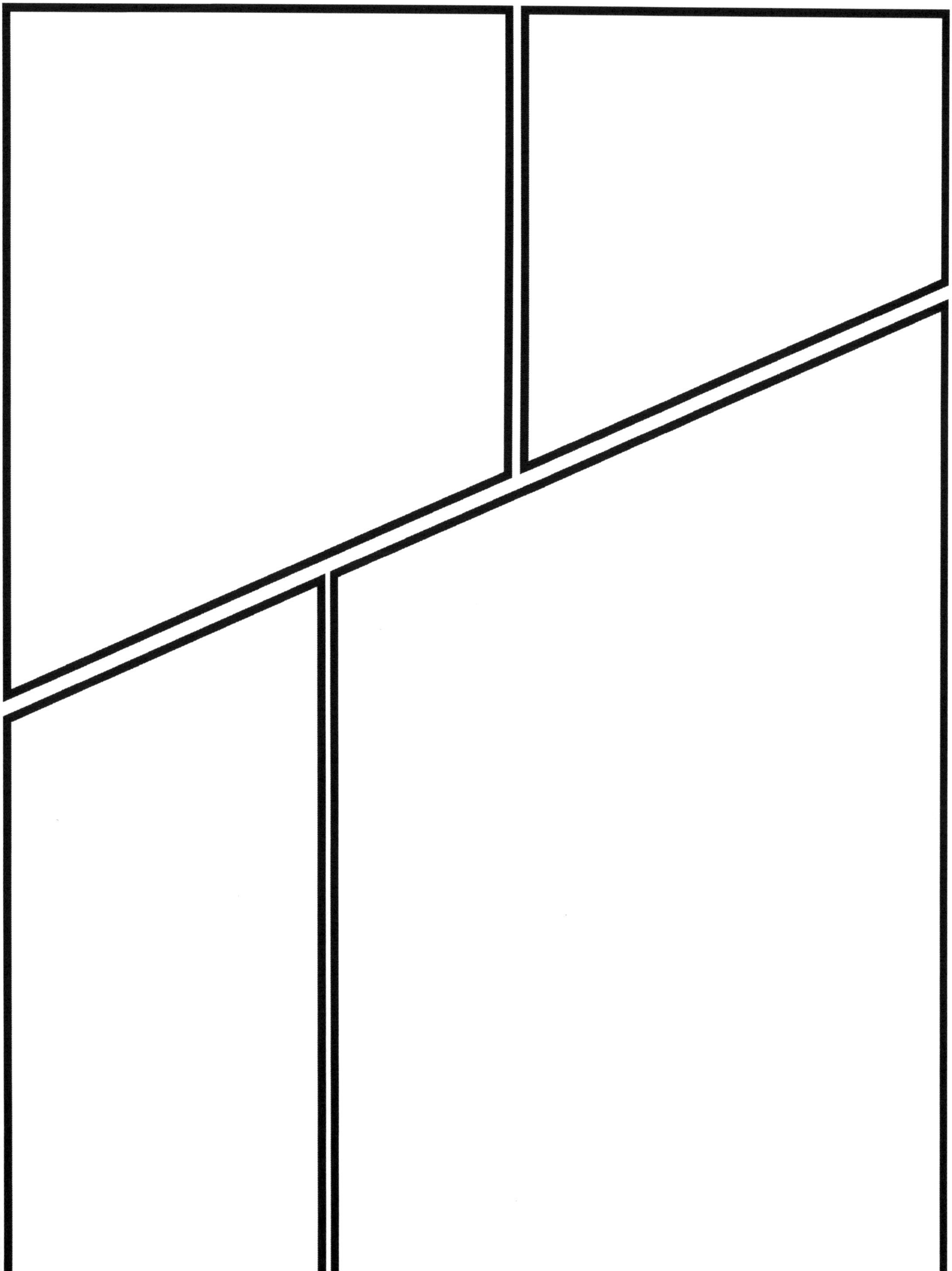

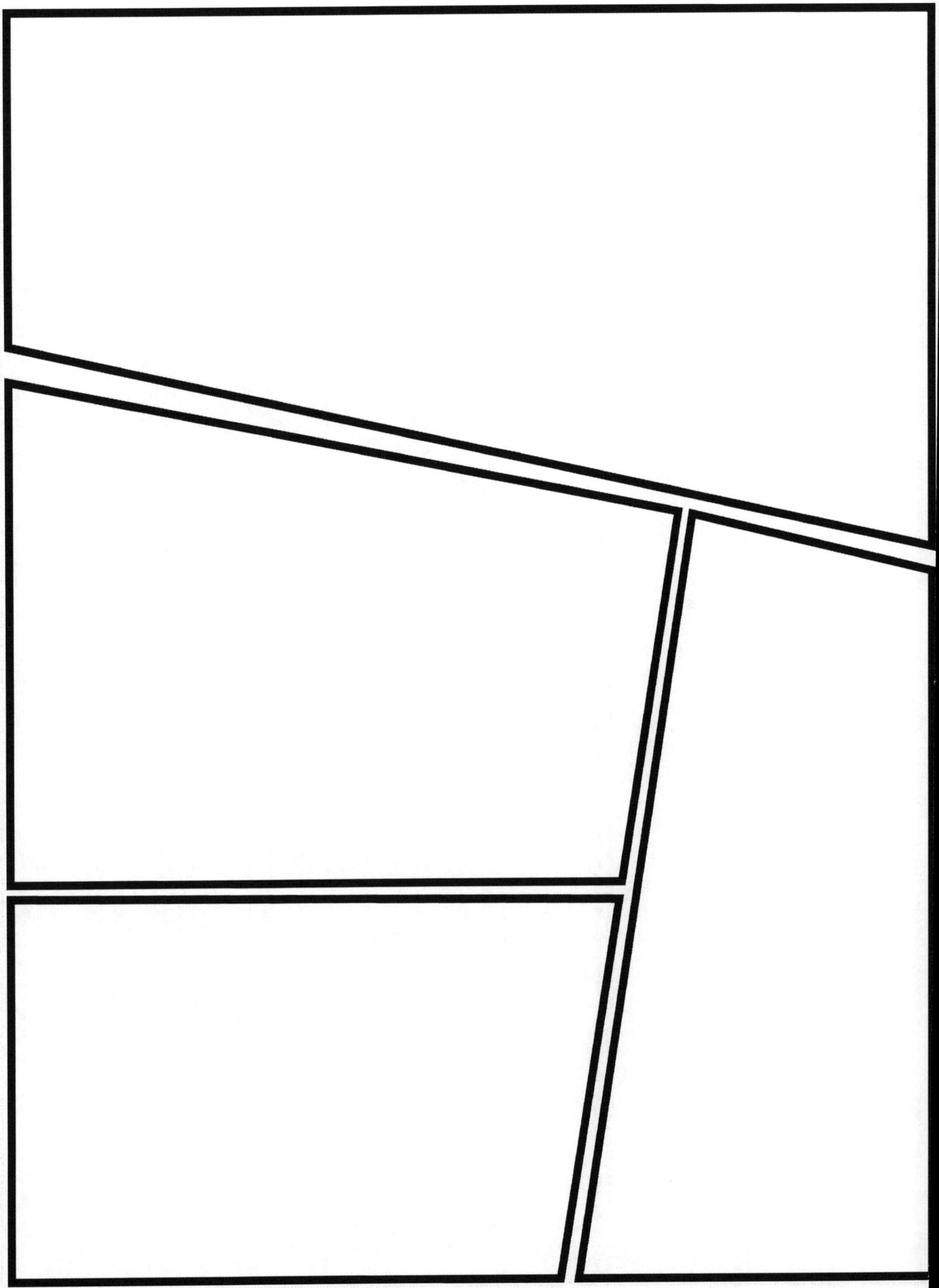

Made in the USA
Coppell, TX
04 July 2021

58555272R00072